# FRENCH
# MODERNE

*Franck Audoux*

# FRENCH
# MODERNE
## COCKTAILS

### FROM THE 1920s & 1930s

**RIZZOLI**
NEW YORK

4

"... The cocktail is not this plus that...
It is a way of adding together. One must
stir... It is the very cocktail creator who
stirs up. The bar's charm comes from
the shaker of elements."

Louis Delluc, *L'homme des bars*. Paris, La Pensée Française, 1923.

# TABLE OF CONTENTS

# A NEW WORLD

6

"I gave the chauffeur the address of a bar on rue Daunou. She raved like a schoolgirl about the bartender's white vest, the grace with which he shook the silver cups, the strange and poetic names of the mixes."

Raymond Radiguet, *Le Diable au Corps*, Paris, Grasset, 1923.

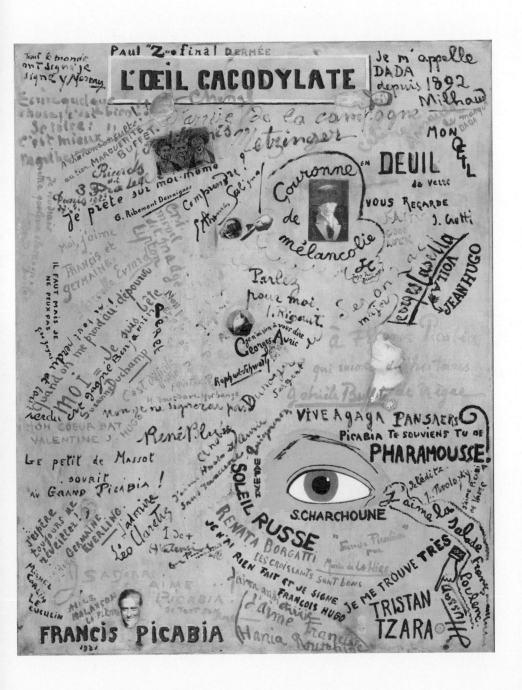

Francis Picabia, *The Cacodylate Eye*, 1921
Signed by Jean Hugo, Milhaud, Poulenc, Pansaers, Soupault...

# THE AGE OF THE AUTOMOBILE, AIRPLANE, COCKTAIL, TELEPHONE, AND WIRELESS TELEGRAPH

On November 11, 1918, France was jubilant, but it was left ravaged by four years of war. The toll of the conflict was terrifying. In addition to those who had died on the field of battle were those who later succumbed to their wounds, or else were permanently mutilated by shrapnel, chemical weapons, and the effects of shellshock. Added to this butcher's bill were innumerable civilian casualties, the victims of famine, and the Spanish flu. Even the very soil had suffered, with untold hectares of farmland ruined by artillery. It was also during this great bloodletting that a commingling of classes occurred in the trenches. In the home front, women began to tackle tasks that were once the preserve of men. The values of a time before the war were called into question—the very values that had triggered the slaughter.

8

In reaction, ten wild years ensued and every form of pleasure was welcomed. It was pleasure intensified by new entertainments, new dress codes, new music, new dance, new artistic approaches, and new drinks. It was a new world. It was a world in which the United States, in its steady march to become the indispensable nation in world affairs, suddenly yoked itself with Prohibition in 1920. It was a world where the Soviet Union was recognized by France in 1924, seven years after the Bolshevik Revolution. It was a world where Italy fell under the spell of Mussolini, and saw the rise of National Socialism in Weimar Germany. The decade of euphoria came to an end the with the stock market crash of 1929. France, caught between what it owed its allies and reparations from Germany, was hit by the crisis a little later, in the early 1930s. Nationalist movements were on the rise, as was the socialist Front Populaire. It was during these troubled times that the cocktail took refuge in luxury hotels where, after the frenzy of the 1920s, it would serve as a reminder of more peaceful times.

"The Victory Celebration",
special issue of *L'Illustration* from July 19, 1919.

*"We will never again see such a spectacle. Because there will be no more war."*[1]

On July 14, 1919, the French army and its allies (with Americans at the fore) paraded through Paris. The streets were flooded with people and soon so were balls, theaters, and bars. It was a victory march that would last a decade, and the hated enemy would be made to pay for it. The victory march propelled France into the new century period.

France looked inwardly, its eyes trained on its own capital, where the optimism of the still-young twentieth century was so rudely interrupted. A new society would blossom in cosmopolitan Paris. All the social classes were represented, and even if they did not mingle, they nevertheless participated in an exchange that encouraged "mixing". Among the foreigners there were businessmen and workers; France was a country that needed to be rebuilt, and Poles were the principal representatives. Paris was the capital of human rights, drawing Russians and, later, Italians fleeing a fascist regime to settle there. Tourists poured into the "capital of victory" and met in bars and cafés. To establish its international influence, Paris would again host the modern Olympic Games, under the aegis of Pierre de Coubertin in 1924. (Another universal exposition would happen much later, in 1937, during which the German and Soviet pavilions would face off on Place du Trocadéro.)

The premise for mass tourism took shape. Tourism was supported both by an infrastructure that adapted itself to the needs of travelers and by increasingly efficient means of transportation. Transatlantic voyages on steamships now took less time. Planes between Paris and London led to the founding of Air France in 1933. The railway continued to develop and facilitate movement throughout the country; it was soon rivaled by the automobile, the symbol of speed and freedom. Speed, already magnified by the Futurists in the columns of *Le Figaro* before the war, become the emblem of the new society. Speed of movement, of rhythm, of innovation and pleasure, was the spirit of the age[2]. Tourism also brought about mass culture. Daily media sources multiplied and documentary photography emerged, leveraging advertising. It was also the beginning of radio, which broadcasted

10

[1] — Maurice Sachs, *Au temps du Bœuf sur le Toit* (Paris: La Nouvelle Revue Critique, 1939).
[2] — "Le Futurisme," *Le Figaro*, February 20, 1909.

The Eiffel Tower, Paris, 1930s.
Anonymous photograph.

concerts and sporting events. It was the height of music hall reviews, and in 1927 movies like *The Jazz Singer* were given sound. Meanwhile, Charlie Chaplin was welcomed with open arms when he visited. French cinema, launched by Louis Delluc, followed suit; directors Marcel L'Herbier, Jean Renoir, and René Clair would exert international influence and discover stars like Charles Boyer.

The city would again be reborn as a cultural capital. The birthplace of Cubism, it was later the hometown of Dada, a diverse movement with international repercussions, and then of Surrealism. The avant-garde, blooming in fine art, literature, and music drew society into a creative frenzy. A new society, in a new world, where the cocktail would play an integral part.

Pages 13, 16–21: Advertisements from 1929-1930.
Pages 14–15: *Manifestation Dada*, Paris, 1920.

# MAISON de L'ŒUVRE

## (Salle Berlioz)

## 55, rue de Clichy

Métro : Clichy — Nord-Sud : Trinité

Le Samedi 27 Mars, à 8 h. 15 précises

# MANIFESTATION DADA

Prix des Places

Fauteuil d'orchestre { Les deux premiers rangs. 20 fr.
{ Autres rangs . . . . . . 10 fr.

Balcon { Les 6 premiers rangs de face. . . 5 frs
{ Autres rangs. . . . . . . . . . 3 fr.

Tous les droits compris

Pour la location s'adresser :

A la Maison de l'Œuvre, Tél. : Gut. 67-31.
Au Sans Pareil, 37, avenue Kléber.
Maison des Amis des Livres, 7, rue de l'Odéon.

programme :

## présentation des dadas

par Mac ROBBER

## le ventriloque désaccordé

parade en un acte de Paul DERMÉE

Personnages : le ventriloque . . .
le marin . . . . . .     le ventriloque Sapin, 3' creux
le soudier . . . . .
une jeune fille . . .     un homme

## pas de la chicorée frisée

G. RIBEMONT-DESSAIGNES

Interprété au piano par Mlle Marguerite Buffet

## dadaphone

par Tristan TZARA

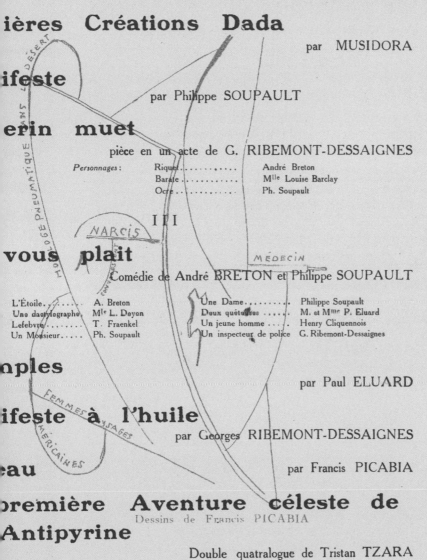

ifeste **cannibale dans l'obscurité**

par André Breton et accompagné au piano par M^lle Marguerite Buffet

Texte et Musique de Francis PICABIA

s **de prestidigitation**

par Louis ARAGON

ières **Créations Dada**

par MUSIDORA

ifeste

par Philippe SOUPAULT

erin **muet**

pièce en un acte de G. RIBEMONT-DESSAIGNES

Personnages :  Riquet............  André Breton
Barate ...........  M^lle Louise Barclay
Ocre.............  Ph. Soupault

III

vous **plait**

Comédie de André BRETON et Philippe SOUPAULT

L'Étoile............  A. Breton      Une Dame.........  Philippe Soupault
Une dactylographe.  M^le L. Deyon   Deux quêteuses .....  M. et M^me P. Eluard
Lefebvre.........  T. Fraenkel     Un jeune homme ....  Henry Cliquennois
Un Monsieur.....  Ph. Soupault    Un inspecteur de police  G. Ribemont-Dessaignes

mples

par Paul ELUARD

ifeste **à l'huile**

par Georges RIBEMONT-DESSAIGNES

eau

par Francis PICABIA

remière **Aventure céleste de**

Dessins de Francis PICABIA

**Antipyrine**

Double quatralogue de Tristan TZARA

u.....'....  Ph. Soupault        M. Antipyrine.......  André Breton
ières ....  Louis Aragon        M. Boumboum, directeur  G. R. D.
enceinte ....  M^lle Céline Arnauld  Npala Garoo .........  Th. Fraenkel
...........  Paul Eluard         Tr. Tzara............  Tr. Tzara

et un manifeste chanté par M^lle Hania ROUTCHINE

VIENT DE PARAITRE : **DADAPHONE** N° 7. PRIX : 1 FR. 50

avec les photographies des Présidents du mouvement Dada

VIENT DE PARAITRE : **391** N° 12. PRIX : 2 FRANCS
VIENT DE PARAITRE : **PROVERBE** N^os 2, 3, 4. PRIX : 0 FR. 50

**DADA** société anonyme pour l'exploitation des idées

Administration : AU SANS PAREIL.

37, Avenue Kléber

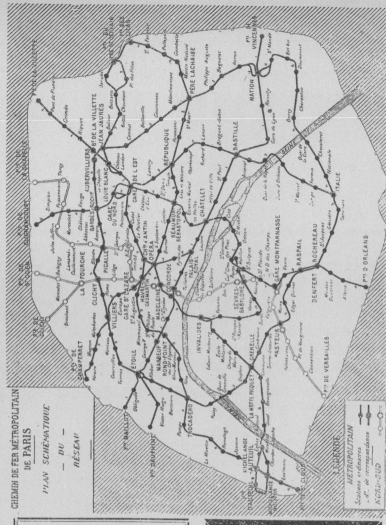

CHEMIN DE FER MÉTROPOLITAIN
DE PARIS
— PLAN SCHÉMATIQUE —
— DU —
RÉSEAU

LÉGENDE
MÉTROPOLITAIN
Stations ordinaires
, d° de correspondance
NORD-SUD

magnifique appareil
**VITUS**
pour votre Salon

— 30 —

# AMERICAN DRINKS

### INTRODUCED BY NAPOLÉON III, LOUIS FOUQUET, AND A FEW OTHERS

It was from his exile in London that Napoléon III introduced to France the word "bar", referring to the wood counter you lean on. And it was after his visit to the first Great Exhibition of 1851 in the Crystal Palace there that he decided a similar exhibition would take place in Paris. These two world's fairs would be milestones of the century's end.

Following the first French iteration, in 1855, the 1867 International Exposition was held at the Champs de Mars. Alongside the principal pavilions, which that year were devoted to Agriculture, the Fine Arts and Industry—with each participating country presenting its jewel—the fair launched the concept of national pavilions as well. On a designated plot, each nation built a pavilion in which it exhibited what it deemed best about its culture, history, and innovations. Forty-two nations were represented, and among the hundreds of cafés and international restaurants it was at the American counter that certain refreshments were all the rage.[1] Young women (the waitress had not yet been replaced by the bartender) served drinks that were sipped cold through small grass straws. American drinks were officially entering the French consciousness.

Although some reports had already championed these beverages, such as Oscar Comettant's 1857 book *Trois ans aux États-Unis*, they could be consumed only in select-cafés. The 1867 exposition was attended by almost fifteen million visitors, and the 1878 fair by more than sixteen million. At the latter, after climbing to the top of the Statue of Liberty, fair visitors could go to the packed American bar, where the sherry cobbler and mint julep were the most popular drinks.[2] The American drink trend was now in full force.

[1] – "L'Exposition de 1867," *La Semaine des Familles*, No.43, July 27, 1867.
[2] – "A travers l'Exposition," *L'Univers Illustré*, No.1220, August 10, 1878.

The first French book of cocktails, titled *Méthode pour composer soi-même les boissons américaines, anglaises, italiennes etc.*, was published on the eve of the 1889 fair celebrating the centennial of the French Revolution. Proposed within were 160 recipes, supplemented by a French-English glossary that answered the most common questions in the food world. The book was meant mainly for café and restaurant owners as well as for maîtres d'hôtel. Its author, Émile Lefeuvre, encouraged those professionals to learn about new drinks in order to properly meet the expectations of foreign visitors coming to Paris to experience the new iron tower that soared some one thousand feet into the sky (the total number of visitors to the Exposition Universelle of 1889 surpassed thirty-two million). A highlight, again, were the so-called Anglo-American bars, with their white-vested waiters, high stools, excellent mixes, and Welsh rarebit.

Louis Fouquet's *Bariana: Recueil pratique de toutes boissons américaines et anglaises*, the second cocktail book in French, was published in 1896. It was sold at the Criterion, named for the London establishment whose proprietors, Spiers and Pond, were also behind the American-style bar and grill room at the 1889 fair. Émile Fouquet, Louis's father, opened the Criterion at 121, rue Saint-Lazare in Paris, across from the Hôtel Terminus, in December 1895. It billed itself as an "English and American Luncheon Bar" that served "American, English and French drinks". On the menu were summer (iced) and winter (hot) drinks, cocktails, long drinks, English beers, port, gin and whiskies, French aperitifs, and more. Prices were between 75 centimes and 1 franc. In the grill room, a dish of the day was on offer for 1 franc 25 centimes: Monday Irish ragout, Thursday hot roast beef, Friday roasted leg of lamb, and veal stew on Saturday; cold cuts, oysters, and cheese were available at all times. Cocktails were on offer by the liter, ready to be served; they could also be delivered for honeymoons and parties.

The Criterion was such a success that a branch was opened in September 1898 at 99, Avenue des Champs-Élysées. Louis was in charge. In addition to the Criterion, there was now Fouquet's Bar, named in the Anglo-Saxon vein, as was its peer, Maxim's.

## RACING MATTERS

*"The Americans started by shortening stirrups. Then our women
slashed their skirts and our girls got rid of their hair."*[3]

Before the war, bars serving English and American drinks were
the exclusive domain of men and for the most part were
frequented by the racing world. Owners, trainers, simple bettors.
Horses were in the air; it was all about racing. And there was no
shortage of conversation subjects in those early years of the 1900s.
The horse world was buzzing with activity. The trend of the so-
called American seat was a true revolution in flat horseracing.
Introduced in Europe by Tod Sloan (of Bunker Hill, Indiana),
the "revelation" of the 1898 horseracing season in England,
his mount caused a sensation. It involved crouching forward over
the horse's neck, with stirrups so short that the jockey's knees
touched the horse's shoulders. Sloan was met with taunts
and jeers when he first raced in France, but owners and trainers
soon heeded the rallying cry to adopt this new technique.
These were the years of American jockeys like Milton Henry,
winner of the Grand Prix de Paris in Longchamp in 1907.
English jockeys, keepers of the flame, were soon ousted by their
victories. The lone Frenchman, Georges Stern, seemed able
to remain standing.

In the heart of Paris, at the Chatam Bar, talk was all about these
American jockeys, fixed races, and the new machine used as
a starting gate.
Located at 17, rue Daunou, the bar of the Hôtel Chatam opened
in 1885. On the outside, a sculpted wood façade and three
stained-glass windows, decorated with the armorials of England,
the United States, and the City of Paris, drew in sportsmen.
Inside, a mahogany bar, specially ordered from New York,
greeted them. As for the walls, they were covered with equestrian
prints. Soon, a grill room adjoining the bar enhanced the new
establishment.
The manager, Santoz, and the bartender, Johnny Mita, turned
the business into *the* pre-race meeting place. The spot was
so reputed that, according to a municipal report from 1910,
cars parked in front waiting to drive their clients to the Bois
de Boulogne caused traffic jams, disrupting horse and buggies

24

[3] — Jean Trarieux, *Si les chevaux pouvaient parler* [If horses could talk]
Paris: Librairie Stock, 1926.

A "New York" Bar in Paris around 1910.
Anonymous photograph.

and automobiles alike.[4] It is in this context that the *ROSE* [P.91] was created for the port-wine and cocktail hour. The talk of the town, this cocktail Rose became the most fashionable of the interwar period. It was so popular that soon every bartender was making his own version.

Nearby, on the much calmer Rue Volney, at number 11, was Henry's Hotel and Henry's Bar, which opened in 1890. The proprietor Henri Tépé was one of the best bartenders at the time; he had helped open the Chatam and also owned racehorses. His clientele, which mostly followed when he left the Chatam, was solely male and all racegoers.
But the story turned tragic. In April 1918, Tépé threw himself out a window. His widow took the reins of the establishment. Was alcohol the problem or was his patriotism called into question, as suggested by the press?[5] Although a naturalized French citizen for over thirty years, Tépé was born in Germany. Rumor had it that he was suspected of espionage and had been arrested on that fateful day.
Yet another jockey's story shaped number 5, Rue Daunou. "Nell" Henry, the eccentric wife of Milton Henry, opened a bar on Thanksgiving Day 1911. It was called the New York Bar, a name that was common and foreshadowed the "Bar Américain". Among its patrons was "Chips" Brighton, a former jockey. In the basement was a cabaret and its piano. Even Tod Sloan joined the venture for a while. Sloan had been thrown out of England after being condescending, with cigar in mouth, to the Prince of Wales (the future Edward VII), or maybe for breaking a bottle of Champagne on the waiter's head in Ascot. In all likelihood, it was for illegal betting, as was often the case with Sloan. He would leave France for good on the eve of World War I, and the New York Bar would become a thing of legend when it was bought by Harry MacElhone in 1923 (see page 130). Between stout and whiskies, one cocktail was very popular during the war, the *75* [P.70]. Its effect was as fierce as the eponymous canon in French field artillery, the pride of the army. The cocktail would appear again much later after victory, as a Champagne cocktail named the *FRENCH 75* [P.70].

26

---

[4] – *Rapport sur la circulation générale des voitures et des piétons à Paris* [Report on the general traffic of cars and pedestrians in Paris] (Conseil Municipal de Paris, 1910).
[5] – "Le Petit Parisien," *Le Soir*, January 21, 1918.

### PARIS, CAPITAL OF AMERICA [6]

To the question posed by the magazine *Transition* "Why do you prefer to live outside America?" Hilaire Hiler answered, "When Albrecht Dürer was asked by letter why he remained so long in Venice he replied, 'Because here I am considered a gentleman; at home a loafer.'"[7]

There were many Americans in Paris. Of course, among them were artists drawn to the French capital's effervescence, those who wanted to escape the Puritanism in their own country. A wide array of literature and painting would reflect their celebrated lives in Paris. There were also many artists who were less productive, the dilettantes.
The avant-garde had its own neighborhood, Montparnasse— "the quarter", as Americans called it—superior to Montmartre, Greenwich Village, and Chelsea.[8] It had its own magazines (*The Little Review, Transition*), and a bookstore, Shakespeare and Co., which was managed by Sylvia Beach, the Anglo-Saxon counterpart to her lover Adrienne Monnier, who ran La Maison des Amis du Livre. This community gathered around a circle of intellectuals, publishers, journalists, and patrons of the arts.
There was also a business community that had its own haunts on the Right Bank, clubs and associations including the powerful American Chamber of Commerce. That disparate community benefited from the institutions devoted to them. The American Hospital of Paris, which opened in 1909, had emerged from the American association three years before and aimed to provide health care to Americans living in or passing through the city, even the poorest among them. The American Library in Paris was founded when the United States entered World War I, and the Sorbonne's American library opened in 1920. The press was not to be overshadowed. The *New York Herald Tribune*, the *Chicago Tribune*, and the *Wall Street Journal* all had offices in Paris. In addition to these residents, there were hordes of tourists who took advantage of a more than favorable exchange rate; legend has it that they would glue French francs onto their suitcases as souvenirs!

[6] – *Paris, capitale de l'Amérique, l'avant-garde américaine à Paris*, catalogue de l'exposition, Musée d'Art Américain Giverny, 2003.
[7] – *Why do Americans live in Europe?*, Transition, No.14, fall 1928.
[8] – Lettre from Marcel Duchamp, in Jimmy Charters *This must be the place*, ed.Herbert Joseph, London, 1934.

As for Prohibition, it came as no surprise to France. General Pershing had already issued a decree during the war prohibiting French businesses from serving alcohol to American soldiers of every rank. The French press delighted in stories about bootleggers and were astonished how easily their reporter, on a trip to New York, was able to find a drink.

Prohibition clearly affected business relationships but it also recruited many bartenders to Paris. The only one who could really complain was the Count Maxence de Polignac. A representative of a Champagne company, Polignac was arrested in New York with seven cases of alcohol, even though he was leaving for France after a business trip to Canada. Accused of smuggling and released on $25,000 bail, he had no intention of returning to the United States for his court date.

### A SENSE OF FRENCH IDENTITY

Is not the cocktail related to the French aperitif? Are not the best cocktails made with the best French liqueurs? Should the word not be spelled *coquetel*?

Considering how important the cocktail had become in society, some were eager to "find" French origins in the phenomenon. Their research would lead them all the way to Napoléon Bonaparte, emperor of the French and a great enthusiast of a Bordeaux recipe already several centuries old that consisted of a mix of wine and eau de vie. Its name was *coquetel*.

But while there was indeed a relationship, it is to the writer Joris-Karl Huysmans that one must turn. In his novel *À rebours*, published in 1884, the character des Esseintes invents a mouth organ. The keys of his organ are connected to the spouts of small liqueur barrels (containing curaçao, gin, and kirsch, for example) that sit side by side, allowing him to compose a gustatory symphony. That is, to create a cocktail.

Beyond fantasies of genealogy, bartenders genuinely considered the particularities of cocktails "à la *française*". Maurice Des Ombiaux, the famous Belgian food critic, mirrored the concern in the press, notably the November 1928 edition of *L'œil de Paris*.

Living in France since the war and a contributor to several newspapers, Des Ombiaux emphasized in each of his reviews

the quality of the cocktails offered by an establishment, and
he championed a gourmet approach. He urged that the bartender
bring spirit and attention to his mix, that he develop it with
the same attention as a chef. The most successful example of such
"French" cocktails was the ROSE [P.91]. The big French liquor brands
would promote the initiative, with varying degrees of enthusiasm,
and not only for mercantile reasons. This cocktail was also
becoming an ambassador of French cultural influence.

Not yoked by Prohibition and with no need to hide, as was then
the case in the United States, the cocktail developed in many
well-established institutions throughout France. The ambiance
and decor were unique at each, from rustic inn to a minimalist,
single-color motif. Of course American drinks were served
at American bars, but they were also served in restaurants, cabarets,
dance halls, and elsewhere. Above all, cocktails developed
in the purely French tradition of the Parisian café. (It was at the Café
de la Paix that Frank Newman, while he worked there,
first mentioned a DRY MARTINI [P.81] in his 1904 book *American Bar*,
which was written in French.) Such cafés and their terraces
perfectly symbolized this period of intellectual and physical
fermentation. Those in Montparnasse were the most exemplary;
sometimes bars and dancing areas were added, gathering
all activities under one roof.
The cocktail had definitively become French!

29

Avenue des Champs-Élysées, Paris, 1930s.
Anonymous photograph.

# "THE COCKTAIL HOUR REPLACED TEA TIME"

### CONTESTS

Far beyond a trend, the cocktail became a genuine societal phenomenon. Its many variations were imbibed everywhere— not one restaurant, dance hall, or cabaret, not one theater or movie house, was without an American bar. The cocktail became the symbol of these festive times, and it was the greatest draw of any occasion. Amid the euphoria, contests emerged and abounded. Among classic competitions for outlandish beauty and elegance (contests for best eye makeup, contests for smokers), the cocktail contest, popular in the late 1920s, was the most championed. Whether amateur matches, in which pretty Parisian celebrities gave new recipes a try, or professional championships that brought together shaker "aces", the public was always the jury and named the Queen of Cocktails and the King Shaker. Such events were guaranteed entertainment that the press, almost always a partner, generously promoted. Liquor brands also were involved, sponsoring the contests and thus benefitting from the publicity.

The wave of contests originated in Biarritz. It was at the Hôtel Miramar that the first one took place, in September 1928. The most aristocratic of the world's beaches attracted the coast's jet set. Next the wave swept into Paris. In the lavish salons of the Hôtel Claridge, the daily *Paris-Midi* and its peer the *Chicago Tribune* invited readers to attend the First International Championship of Cocktails, sponsored by the newspapers. Amateurs and professionals faced off at small wooden bars, and an eager public came to sample their concoctions.

The crowd bombarded "Miss France". A tall brunette with grey-green eyes, Mademoiselle Raymonde Allain had returned from America and the International Beauty Contest in Galveston, Texas, which had ranked her the second most beautiful woman in the world, after Miss Chicago.[1] She linked arms with Maurice de Waleffe,

[1] – "La deuxième beauté du monde," *Le Journal*, June 13, 1928.

32

head of *Paris-Midi* and president of the jury of the French champion.
The singer and actress Mistinguett, amid applause, made a brief
appearance. Princess Doudjam, who performed with Louis Delluc,
won the grand prize with her *DERNIER ROUND* [P.68], and Raymonde
Latour, the famous fashion journalist in love with speed, won first
prize for *SIX-CYLINDRES* [P.93].

The Championship of Professional Bartenders followed
at the Théâtre Apollo and is remembered for its more than one
thousand visitors, forty cocktails, and a few frictions.
Next came the Cocktail Championship of Luna Park Dancers.
Each of the twenty-eight bars was managed by a bartender
and two star barmaids. The cocktails proved to be more fearsome
than roller coasters. The painters Tsuguharu Foujita and
Kees van Dongen were members of the honorary jury. In the
afternoon, Assolant, Lefèvre, and Loti (but without Schreiber!)
came to sign autographs. Departing from Maine, they followed
Lindbergh on board their plane named *L'oiseau canari*, which
was then exhibited at the Place des Tuileries.
Afterward, there were cocktail contests involving movie stars,
filmmakers, directors... Back along the coast, the Riviera, in the early
1930s, it was in Juan-les-Pins that contests first launched
by Florence Gould would become the highlight of casino terraces.
The appointment of the Shaker Queen drew some twenty
candidates, all in pajamas, of course[2].

33

[2] – "L'élection de la reine du shaker," *Comoedia*, August 27, 1931.

## THE HOME BAR

The American drink became a domestic French custom too.
Cocktails were widely consumed, and they were also widely made.
Shakers were part of every contest in bars and could be found
in homes as well. The cocktail hour replaced teatime.
Instead of a traditional 5 p.m. to 7 p.m. timeframe, friends were
now invited to drinks parties between 6 p.m. and 9 p.m.
Residences came equipped with apartment bars. Every living
room needed something to carry the bottles and equipment
required for offering guests a homemade *ROSE* [P.91] or *MARTINI* [P.81].

It was all part of a delicate staging. Paris's Maison du Cocktail
was the busiest purveyor of home bars on the market. In its store
at 83, rue de la Boétie, it presented an entire line of apartment
bars. Corner bars, office bars, library bars, metal bars… there
was even a collection specially decorated by the artist Paul Colin,
exhibited in a Parisian gallery. Among the various models,
the most successful was undoubtedly the Prince of Wales bar.
A pretty piece that could be tucked away, its function was discreet.
Once opened, the bar presented all the bottles and accessories
needed for making cocktails. Another sought-after model was
the cocktail cellar, which also had all the required elements but
was much smaller and therefore easily moved about.
A similar item, made in England, became a favorite Christmas gift,
the "Cocktails Baby Bar". The portable mahogany case contained
seven liquor bottles, a shaker, mixing glass, bar spoon, and zesting
knife. It included a short manual to aid the recipient in becoming
the perfect bartender.

If so desired, one could buy a single set or cocktail accessory
developed by the most prestigious French companies. Christofle
and Baccarat were purveyors to the chicest establishments,
and the products of Lancel, from cigarette holders to travel items,
proved to be a standard-bearer of the times. You could go
to the famous Parisian department stores, such as the Galeries
Lafayette, La Samaritaine, and Le Bon Marché, at whose
American bar you could have a drink served by Maurice, who had
just finished the summer season at the Domaine de la Corne-
Biche, near Fontainebleau. You might remember to buy those tiny
napkins in different shapes, with their motifs in pink, green,

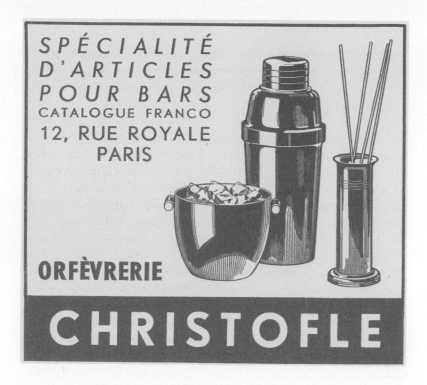

Advertisement for bar accessories
Orfèvrerie Christofle, 1930.

or blue. Or those little forks for skewering olives and cherries
at the bottom of the glass. They are prettiest when topped by
a small colored ball. Unless you prefer the porcelain set—its shaker
depicts a Scottish golf player and the straw case displays a caddy.
Or maybe that small three-liquor keg with three spouts...
Clients with more means would enlist their architects to build
private bars in the art deco style, true American bars with a counter
and stools, but on a smaller scale.
No matter what one chose, the goal was the same. As *Vogue* directed
readers, "Let's make cocktails!"[3]

[3] – "Faisons des cocktails," *Vogue*, December 1, 1926.

## LA GARÇONNE

In 1908 Paul Poiret eliminated the corset. In 1917 Coco Chanel cut off her hair and decided to liberate women from the pre-war silhouette, protesting that "woman [was] only a pretext for riches, lace, sable, chinchilla and overly precious materials".[4]

Women were emancipated through clothing. They broke out of garments, the social armatures of a period that, after four years of war, was now the past. A thirst for independence and freedom took hold of women of the 1920s. They yearned for social and physical independence, freedom of movement. Adrienne Bolland, Suzanne Lenglen, Gaby Morlay, and Joséphine Baker were the heroines of the day.
The war had created a new world and new codes.
Hair was short, and skirts shrank as well. The look was masculine. Cigarette holders and cocktails were must-have accessories. *Garçonne* was a freshly coined word, describing a new type of boyish-looking woman. Victor Marguerite's novel *La garçonne*, published in 1922, proved to be scandalous, which is what made it a top seller (in just a few months, more than one hundred thousand copies were sold). His main protagonist, Monique Lerbier, a worldly and educated woman, rebels against the laws and conventions of her milieu. She clashes with male authority, with a fiancé who has cheated on her, and with parents who see her marriage only from the perspective of their own financial interests. In this psychological novel, scandal comes of her depravity; it is the result of her revolt, sexual freedom, Sapphism, and addiction. Such taboo subjects caused Marguerite to be removed from the Order of the Legion of Honor. Just like Raymond Radiguet, who was criticized for having written in *Le diable au corps* that the war was "four years of holiday".[5] But massive and radical revolt was needed to break out of the shackles of hundreds of years.

The *garçonne* is the main character in *L'heure du cocktail*. She is named Balbine. The book, which was published in 1927, is a collection of recipes for each hour of the day. The narrator draws on them to introduce Balbine to the art of drinking. "Allow me to tell you in passing, not only do you all have the same too short dress and the same [*pot à feu sur le front*], but also

---

4 – Paul Morand, *L'allure de Chanel* (Paris: Herman, 1976).
5 – Raymond Radiguet, *Le diable au corps* (Paris: Grasset, 1923).

...et un bar chez le couturier à la mode.

*A Bar at the Fashion House*
Watercolor by Sem, 1928.

equally bad clothing style and equally bad taste in your choice
of lovers and cocktails."[6]
Regardless, the postwar woman went out to restaurants, the movies,
the cabaret and dance halls; yet "Le Bar" was still mostly off limits.
So she made cocktails at home. Women's magazines were teeming
with articles on subtle mixes. *Vogue* collected recommendations
for hosting a dinner or cocktail party;[7] the magazine *Femina* would
not be outdone. As for *La Ruche*, it published readers' letters from
the "French Woman", sharing advice and recipes.
Cocktails played a part in the need for freedom during these heady
times. As Marguerite declares in *La garçonne*: "The elite will
lead the mass. All women carry a force for good inside,
a potential... the power of peace, justice and benevolence. A force
that will bloom!"[8]

6 – Marcel Requien and Lucien Farnoux-Reynaud, *L'heure du cocktail*
(Paris: Société Mutuelle, 1927).
7 – *Vogue*, February, 1933.
8 – Victor Marguerite, *La garçonne* (Paris: Flammarion, 1922), n.p.

## COCKTAILS:
## THE NEW
## EVIL

Paul Reboux's 1930 statement regarding cocktails was categorical:
"The cocktail is an offense to taste and to good taste."[1]
More virulently, in a September 24, 1931, article in *Comoedia*,
he added: "In truth, all the snobs who recommend cocktails,
the writers who endlessly publish cocktail recipes, the extravagant
characters who build cocktail bars into their living room closets
should be hunted down by the vice squad like cocaine and heroin
dealers. They are criminals, public poison, deceitful and smiling
assassins, even more dangerous than the others because they
inspire less mistrust."

Meetings and lectures multiplied, the question was posed: were
you for or against the cocktail? But the trial was without appeal.
A matter of taste? Not that simple. The cocktail had many critics,
and slander abounded.
There were gastronomical grievances. For example, the Prince
of Gastronomy, Curnonsky[2], the famous food critic for whom
the cocktail "was at once a medication, a toothpaste and an explosive",
was a fervent opponent. How could one appreciate good
and healthy French cuisine after drinking three or four of those
industrial mixes that saturated the palate? The trashcan of liquors,
the jazz of alcohols, those uncouth beverages of tainted
alcohol, since America was dry, mixed according to barbaric
recipes, could not but offend fine French taste. French because
it involved France.
There were other grievances at a time when nationalism filled
more and more chests with pride. The cocktail was not a French
beverage. Imported from America, consumed out of snobbery,
the cocktail was part of the Americanization of French society,
like cigarettes and jazz. It compromised the prestige of France
and threatened commercial prosperity. For was not a glass of wine
the best cocktail, and was not the cocktail the most fearsome
enemy of French wine? In a city where only English was now heard,[3]

38

[1] – Paul Reboux *Le nouveau savoir-vivre* (Paris, Flammarion, 1930).

[2] – Curnowsky was the pen-name of Maurice Edmond Sailland.

[3] – "Le Français tel qu'on le parle," *Le Petit Parisien*, September 3, 1921.

the French bar had to tackle the situation and stop its American counterpart. As patriots, it was one's duty to defend the national wine-producing industry.

Georges Guillain, head of neurology at the Hôpital de la Salpêtrière in Paris, issued a medical warning during the April 30, 1929, session of the Academy of Medicine: the consumption of cocktails led to alcoholism; cocktail addicts suffered from digestive and heart issues, nervous disorders and epilepsy.
The plague of the Belle Époque, alcoholism returned to haunt French society. Absinthe was replaced by the cocktail, common people by the wealthy class. New evil, new name, high-society alcoholism was genuinely dangerous because it affected the elites, the working, educated youth of a country that was already down in the trenches. Women, the top consumers of this poison, brought it into their homes, to their living room bars, where it degenerated young generations and endangered the future of the entire nation.

To confront this new evil, the wine industry once again organized— for it had already faced down the "*fée verte*"—and launched a campaign promoting "national preference", which was widely supported by the newspaper *La Revue du Sommelier*. The finest example was the series of illustrated leaflets by Paul Iribe that Maison Nicolas published annually between 1930 and 1932. (The wine retailer had just started a series of catalogues of luxury price lists illustrated by poster artists like Loupot and Cassandre. Iribe, who began his career with Paul Poiret, had recently returned from the United States, where he worked with Cecil B. DeMille). The first one was entitled *Blanc et Rouge*, which presented different ways of appreciating wine. Next came *Bleu Blanc Rouge*— eminently political, it satirized whiskey, beer, and vodka as well as the countries that produced them. Last was *Rose et Noir*, a virulent plea against the cocktail.[4] Iribe's blurry photographs, silk-screened and enhanced with white gouache, recount a young couple's encounter with the "evil genie" from across the Atlantic.

[4] — René Benjamin, *Rose et Noir*, drawings by Paul Iribe (Paris: Draeger, Paris, 1931).

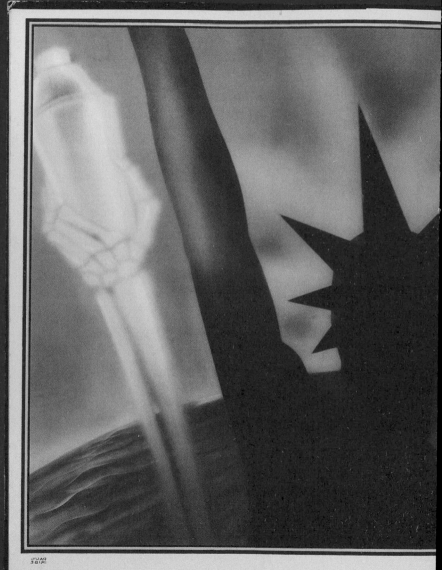

40

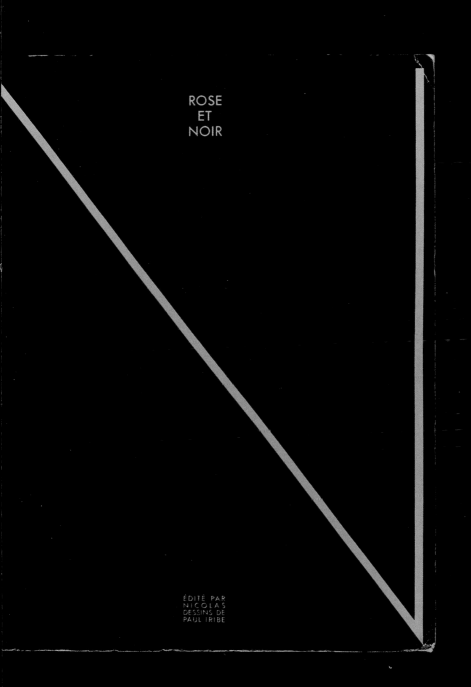

ROSE
ET
NOIR

ÉDITÉ PAR
NICOLAS
DESSINS DE
PAUL IRIBE

*Rose et Noir*, brochure No.2. *The Evil Spirit*, designed by Paul Iribe, published by Nicolas, Paris, 1931.

# 60 RECIPES

"As was his habit, he stopped by the bar at the Ritz where he drank a martini among the sons of American families and high-end crooks."

Pierre Drieu La Rochelle, *Le feu follet*, 1931.

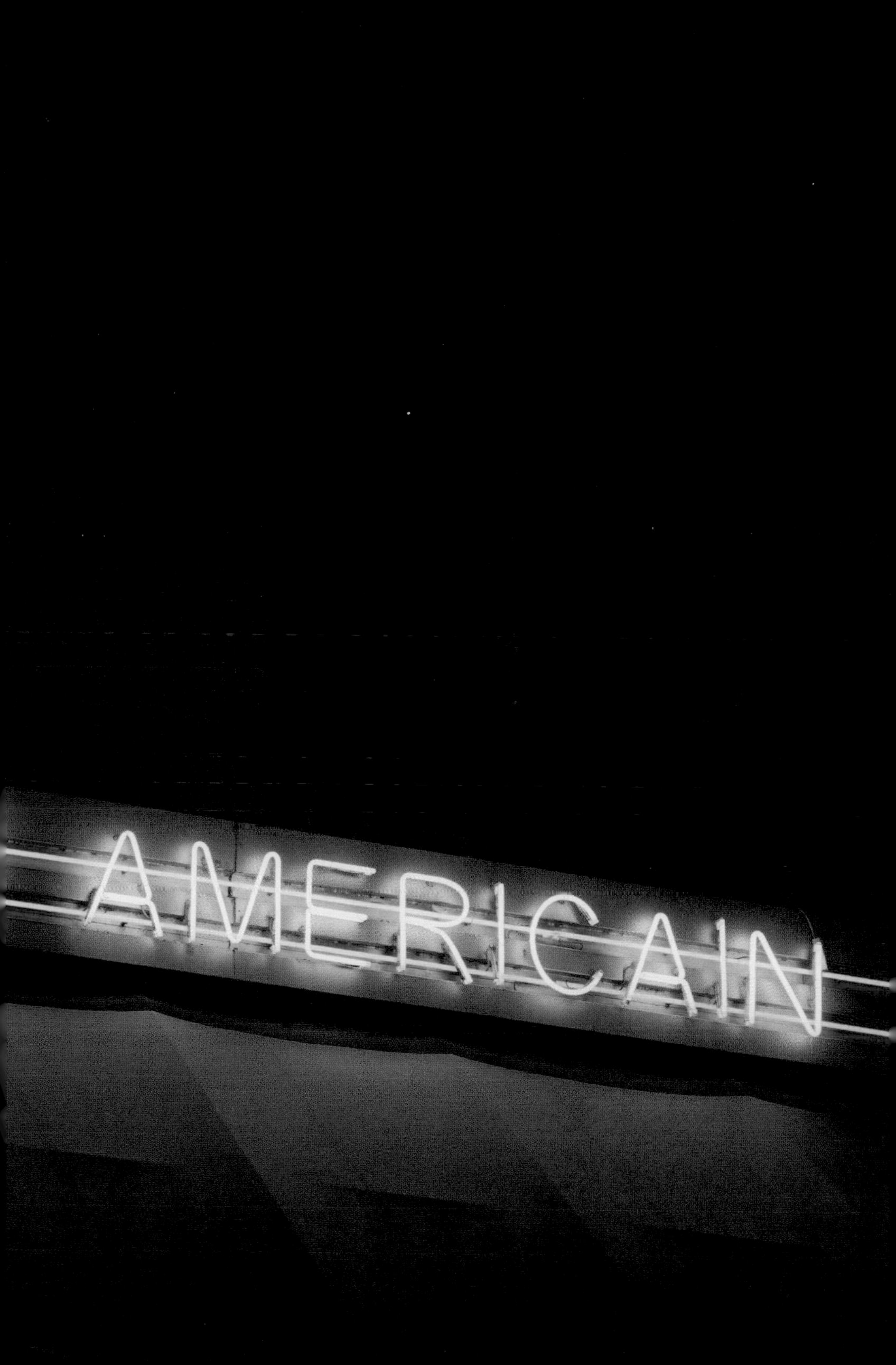
AMERICAIN

## ALASKA

*One of the era's most popular cocktails. The original recipe calls for one part Chartreuse to two parts gin. Be spare with measurements.*

| | |
|---|---|
| *London dry gin* | 50 M | 1 ¾ OZ |
| *Yellow Chartreuse* | 15 ML | ½ OZ |

Stir the ingredients in a shaker tin over ice for fifteen seconds. Strain and serve in a small chilled coupe.

48

## ALEXANDER

CREAM AND CACAO...

*"So smooth and innocent in color, its seductive fire is concealed", as is Ollé's.*

| | |
|---|---|
| *Cognac* | 40 ML | 1 ⅓ OZ |
| *Chocolate liqueur* | 20 ML | ⅔ OZ |
| *Cream* | 20 ML | ⅔ OZ |

Combine the ingredients in a shaker over ice and shake for ten seconds. Double strain and serve in a small chilled cocktail glass.

# ALFONSO

*His Highness Alfonso XIII's favorite drink when he was in Deauville in the early 1920s. This cocktail would become very popular in that Normandy resort town.*

| | |
|---:|:---|
| *White sugar* | 1 CUBE |
| *Angostura bitters* | |
| *Dubonnet* | 30 ML \| 1 OZ |
| *Champagne for topping* | 90 ML \| 3 OZ |
| *Lemon twist* | |

Place the sugar cube saturated with bitters at the bottom of a champagne flute. Add Dubonnet (French wine aperitif with peels, quinine, and orange) and top with Champagne. Stir, squeeze lemon twist and garnish.

49

# BACARDI

*Although the first recipes for this cocktail combined gin and Santiago de Cuba rum, they soon became grenadine daiquiris.*

| | |
|---:|:---|
| *Bacardi rum* | 50 ML \| 1 ¾ OZ |
| *Lime juice* | 25 ML \| ⅞ OZ |
| *Grenadine* | 15 ML \| ½ OZ |

Place the ingredients in a shaker over ice and shake for twenty seconds. Strain twice and serve in a small chilled glass.

## BAISER D'AMOUR

*Inspired by Jean Lupoiu's recipe, this is actually a twist of an Alexander with Grand Marnier, the French orange cognac liqueur created in 1880. The author mentions in his book* 370 Cocktail Recipes *that because it was so difficult to find sour cream and fresh milk in Indochina, he used Nestlé condensed milk instead. (Don't try it.)*

| | |
|---|---|
| *Grand Marnier* | 40 ML \| 1 ⅓ OZ |
| *Cream* | 40 ML \| 1 ⅓ OZ |
| *Cacao bitters* | 3 DASHES |

Combine the ingredients in a shaker over ice and shake for ten seconds. Double strain and serve in a small chilled cocktail glass.

## B & B

THE DIGESTIF COCKTAIL PAR EXCELLENCE.

*Invented at New York's 21 Club, Bénédictine's U.S. representative convinced the company to market its own bottled mix.*

| | |
|---|---|
| *Cognac* | 30 ML \| 1 OZ |
| *Bénédictine* | 30 ML \| 1 OZ |

Stir the ingredients in a shaker tin over ice for fifteen seconds. Strain and serve in a small chilled coupe.

Bénédictine advertisement, 1935.

A.M. Cassandre, "Dubonnet", *L'Illustration*, 1935.

# BARBARESQUE

*Loosely inspired by Paul Colin's recipe, which originally included only rum, Cointreau, and lemon.*

| | |
|---|---|
| *Pineapple rum* | 50 ML \| 1 ¾ OZ |
| *Lime juice* | 25 ML \| ⅞ OZ |
| *Cointreau* | 10 ML \| ⅓ OZ |
| *Falernum* | 10 ML \| ⅓ OZ |
| *Egg white* | 20 ML \| ⅔ OZ |
| *Nutmeg* | |
| *Cinnamon* | |

Combine the ingredients in a shaker without ice and shake vigorously for fifteen seconds. Add ice and shake again for fifteen seconds. Double strain and serve in a large chilled coupe. Sprinkle with grated nutmeg and cinnamon.

53

# BEES KNEE'S

FRANK MEIER'S CLASSIC.

*Taste will vary depending on the honey.*

| | |
|---|---|
| *London dry gin* | 50 ML \| 1 ¾ OZ |
| *Lemon juice* | 20 ML \| ⅔ OZ |
| *Honey syrup* | 20 ML \| ⅔ OZ |
| *Lemon twist* | |

Combine the ingredients in a shaker over ice and shake for ten seconds. Double strain and serve in a large chilled coupe. Squeeze lemon twist and garnish.

## BIRIBI

*Introduced by Lucien Gaudin, this Dubonnet cocktail is in equal parts of gin and Dubonnet. From the original recipe he replaced the bitters with Grand Marnier.*
*Gaudin, an Olympic medalist, was on the scene in Deauville and Cannes and must have known Fred Martin, for this is the same recipe as the latter's SAINTE URSULE.*

| | |
|---|---|
| *London dry gin* | 30 ML \| ⅞ OZ |
| *Dubonnet* | 30 ML \| ⅞ OZ |
| *Grand Marnier* | 2.5 ML \| ⅛ OZ |
| *Orange twist* | |

Stir the ingredients in a shaker tin over ice for fifteen seconds. Strain and serve in a chilled aperitif glass. Squeeze a twist of orange and discard.

## BŒUF SUR LE TOIT

*There were many recipes named after this famous cabaret. Here's one from the time of rue Boissy-d'Anglas.*

| | |
|---|---|
| *London dry gin* | 40 ML \| 1 ⅓ OZ |
| *Italian vermouth* | 20 ML \| ⅔ OZ |
| *Cointreau* | 10 ML \| ⅓ OZ |
| *Orange twist* | |

Stir the ingredients in a shaker tin over ice for fifteen seconds. Strain and serve in a chilled aperitif glass. Squeeze orange twist and garnish.

55

*The French Liqueur of American Bars,* advertisement, 1937.

RELAIS PLAZA - RESTAURAN

- 21, AVENUE MONTAIGNE, PARIS

Relais Plaza, Paris, postcard, 1937.

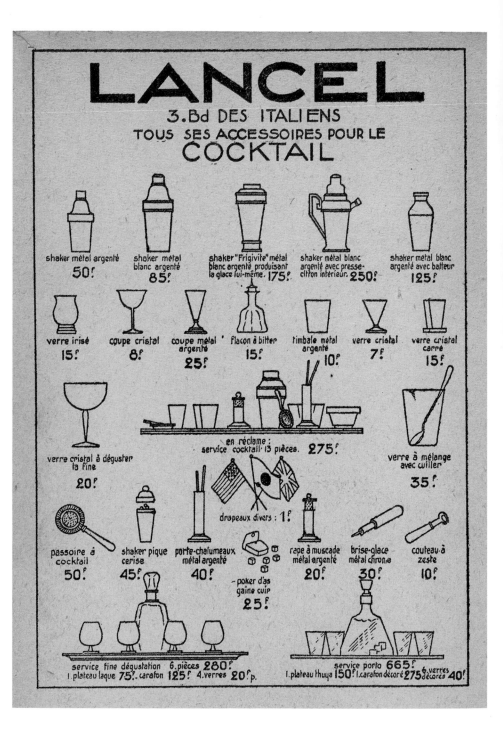

Advertisement for bar accessories, Lancel, 1930.

# BOULEVARDIER

*The cocktail that immortalized* The Boulevardier *magazine.*

| | |
|---|---|
| *Bourbon* | 30 ML \| 1 OZ |
| *Italian vermouth* | 30 ML \| 1 OZ |
| *Campari* | 30 ML \| 1 OZ |
| *Orange twist* | |

Stir the ingredients in a shaker tin over ice for fifteen seconds. Strain and serve in a chilled aperitif glass. Squeeze orange twist and garnish.

# BOULEVARDIER
## COCKTAIL DE PARIS

*This version was inspired by Robert Carme's recipe when he was at Bar Viel. Carme had studied mathematics and wanted to be an engineer, but this version has been simplified.*

| | |
|---|---|
| *Cognac* | 30 ML \| 1 OZ |
| *Dubonnet* | 30 ML \| 1 OZ |
| *Dolin bitters* | 30 ML \| 1 OZ |
| *Orange twist* | |

Stir the ingredients in a shaker tin over ice for fifteen seconds. Strain and serve in a chilled aperitif glass. Squeeze orange twist and garnish.

## BRONX

*Another classic of the era. The first of many recipes to use orange juice.*

| | |
|---|---|
| *London dry gin* | 40 ML \| 1 ⅓ OZ |
| *Italian vermouth* | 15 ML \| ½ OZ |
| *French vermouth* | 15 ML \| ½ OZ |
| *Orange juice* | 15 ML \| ½ OZ |
| *Orange twist* | |

Combine the ingredients in a shaker over ice and shake for fifteen seconds. Double strain and serve in a large chilled coupe. Squeeze orange twist and garnish.

## BYRRH

*Not to be confused with the Byrrh cocktail consisting of equal parts French vermouth, Byrrh, and rye whiskey. This cocktail was invented by Frank Meier, who published the recipe in* The Artistry of Mixing Drinks.

| | |
|---|---|
| *Byrrh* | 40 ML \| 1 ⅓ OZ |
| *Cognac* | 30 ML \| 1 OZ |
| *Kirsch* | 15 ML \| ½ OZ |
| *Brandied cherry* | |

Stir the ingredients in a shaker tin over ice for fifteen seconds. Strain and serve in a chilled aperitif glass. Garnish.

*BARBARESQUE* P.53

## BYRRH-CASSIS

*One of the most popular aperitifs of the interwar period. Traditionally mixed with sparkling water, this version is stronger.*

| | |
|---:|:---|
| *Byrrh* | 50 ML \| 1 ¾ OZ |
| *Crème de cassis* | 10 ML \| ⅓ OZ |

Stir the ingredients in a shaker tin over ice for fifteen seconds. Strain and serve in a chilled aperitif glass.

## BYRRH-C

*Very loosely inspired by the traditional Byrrh-Cassis mixed with sparkling water.*

| | |
|---:|:---|
| *Byrrh* | 50 ML \| 1 ¾ OZ |
| *Triple sec* | 20 ML \| ⅔ OZ |
| *Lemon juice* | 20 ML \| ⅔ OZ |
| *Crème de cassis* | 5 ML \| ⅙ OZ |
| *Sparkling water* | |
| *Lemon twist* | |

Combine the ingredients in a tall glass. Fill with ice and top with sparkling water. Add twist and garnish.

Byrrh advertisement, 1930s.

A.M. Cassandre, *Wagon Bar*, 1932.

## CHARLIE PIE

*The ingredients are the same as a Negroni, but this version is more robust (a Negroni is made with equal parts).*
*Lucien Gaudin dedicated this cocktail to Charlie Rola, bartender at the Cheval Pie.*

| | |
|---|---|
| *London dry gin* | 40 ML \| 1 ⅓ OZ |
| *Italian vermouth* | 30 ML \| 1 OZ |
| *Campari* | 10 ML \| ⅓ OZ |

Stir the ingredients in a shaker tin over ice for fifteen seconds. Strain and serve in a chilled aperitif glass.

65

## CÔTE D'ÉMERAUDE

*Gets its color from Izarra, the Basque liquor. Izarra liqueurs, both green and yellow, are a blend of plants, spices, prunes, and Armagnac. The name says it all. It's the "star" of French Basque country.*
*Rémy and Gaston, from the Bœuf sur le Toit, contributed this cocktail to the book* Cocktails de Paris.

| | |
|---|---|
| *London dry gin* | 20 ML \| ⅔ OZ |
| *Armagnac* | 20 ML \| ⅔ OZ |
| *Green Izarra* | 20 ML \| ⅔ OZ |

Stir the ingredients in a shaker tin over ice for fifteen seconds. Strain and serve in a chilled aperitif glass.

## COUPOLE COCKTAIL

*One of Bob's recipes!*

| | |
|---:|:---|
| *London dry gin* | 40 ML \| 1 ⅓ OZ |
| *Italian vermouth* | 30 ML \| 1 OZ |
| *Calvados* | 10 ML \| ⅓ OZ |

Stir the ingredients in a shaker tin over ice for fifteen seconds. Strain and serve in a chilled aperitif glass.

## DEMPSEY

*The fight of the century, which took place in Jersey City on July 2, 1921, was between Jack Dempsey and Georges Carpentier, the first French light-heavyweight world champion, who had won his title the previous year. The fight was broadcast over American radio and the winner was announced across the Atlantic. Dempsey prevailed. Carpentier retired in 1926; boosted by his popularity, he later opened a bar in Paris. Fred Martin invented this cocktail in Deauville in 1922.*

| | |
|---:|:---|
| *Calvados* | 40 ML \| 1 ⅓ OZ |
| *London dry gin* | 20 ML \| ⅔ OZ |
| *Grenadine* | 5 ML \| ⅙ OZ |
| *Absinthe* | 2.5 ML \| ⅛ OZ |

Stir the ingredients in a shaker tin over ice for fifteen seconds. Strain and serve in a chilled aperitif glass.

*COUPOLE COCKTAIL* <sup>P.66</sup>

## DERNIER ROUND

*Continuing the theme of boxing, this cocktail was invented by Mademoiselle Doudjam, who won the Paris-Midi cup at the Hôtel Claridge's amateur championship. A rising star of the new talkies, she was a better actress than a barmaid. But that didn't stop this recipe from appearing as the Last Round in an edition of Harry MacElhone's* ABC of Mixing Cocktails.

| | |
|---|---|
| *London dry gin* | 40 ML \| 1 ⅓ OZ |
| *Italian vermouth* | 20 ML \| ⅔ OZ |
| *Cointreau* | 10 ML \| ⅓ OZ |
| *Cognac* | 10 ML \| ⅓ OZ |
| *Lemon twist* | |

Stir the ingredients in a shaker tin over ice for fifteen seconds. Strain and serve in a chilled aperitif glass. Squeeze lemon twist and garnish.

## FIOUPE

*Louis Fioupe was spirits agent in Nice. This cocktail was originally prepared with Cinzano's Italian vermouth, which Fioupe represented along the Côte d'Azur. Figure on the Riviera, this cocktail was dedicated to him and became widely popular at the end of the 1920s.*

| | |
|---|---|
| *Cognac* | 30 ML \| 1 OZ |
| *Italian vermouth* | 25 ML \| ⅞ OZ |
| *Bénédictine* | 10 ML \| ⅓ OZ |
| *Brandied cherry* | |
| *Lemon twist* | |

Stir the ingredients in a shaker tin over ice for fifteen seconds. Strain and serve in a chilled digestif glass. Squeeze lemon twist and garnish.

## FORUM COCKTAIL

*A twist on a martini with Grand Marnier.*

| | |
|---|---|
| *London dry gin* | 25 ML \| ⅞ OZ |
| *French vermouth* | 25 ML \| ⅞ OZ |
| *Grand Marnier* | 10 ML \| ⅓ OZ |

Stir the ingredients in a shaker tin over ice for twenty seconds. Strain and serve in a small chilled coupe.

## FRANCE COCKTAIL

### AN INTERPRETATION OF THE B&B, HERE MEANING BRANDY AND BYRRH

*This promotional cocktail could be found in brochures like* Les bonnes recettes de Byrrh, *published by the company in 1939, which combined cooking and cocktail recipes.*

| | |
|---|---|
| *Cognac* | 40 ML \| 1 ⅓ OZ |
| *Byrrh* | 40 ML \| 1 ⅓ OZ |

Stir the ingredients in a shaker tin over ice for fifteen seconds. Strain and serve in a chilled digestif glass.

# FRENCH 75

*The "75" cocktail during the war was made with gin and Calvados. Peacetime turned it into a Champagne cocktail, but it was just as effective. Here is Frank Meier's recipe.*

| | |
|---|---|
| London dry gin | 30 ML \| 1 OZ |
| Lemon juice | 15 ML \| ½ OZ |
| Simple syrup | 15 ML \| ½ OZ |
| Absinthe | 1.25 ML \| 1⁄24 OZ |
| Champagne | |

Combine all ingredients except the Champagne in a shaker and shake for ten seconds. Double strain and serve in a tall glass over ice. Top with Champagne.

# GIN FIZZ

*Another classic from the interwar period, but without the egg white at the time.*

| | |
|---|---|
| London dry gin | 50 ML \| 1 ¾ OZ |
| Lemon juice | 25 ML \| 7⁄8 OZ |
| Simple syrup | 25 ML \| 7⁄8 OZ |
| Sparkling water | |

Combine the ingredients in a shaker over ice and shake for fifteen seconds. Double strain and serve in a tall glass. Top with sparkling water.

Bar Napoléon, Arcades des Champs-Élysées, Paris, postcard, 1932.

## GRATTE-CIEL

*Cocktail invented by Cointreau in the early 1930s.*

| | |
|---|---|
| *Cointreau* | 20 ML \| ⅔ OZ |
| *London dry gin* | 20 ML \| ⅔ OZ |
| *Italian vermouth* | 20 ML \| ⅔ OZ |
| *Cognac* | 10 ML \| ⅓ OZ |
| *Cherry liqueur* | 10 ML \| ⅓ OZ |
| *Orange twist* | |

Stir the ingredients in a shaker tin over ice for fifteen seconds. Strain and serve in a chilled aperitif glass. Squeeze orange twist and garnish.

74

## GREEN HAT

| | |
|---|---|
| *London dry gin* | 30 ML \| 1 OZ |
| *Get* | 30 ML \| 1 OZ |

Stir the ingredients in a shaker tin over ice for fifteen seconds. Strain and serve in a small chilled coupe.

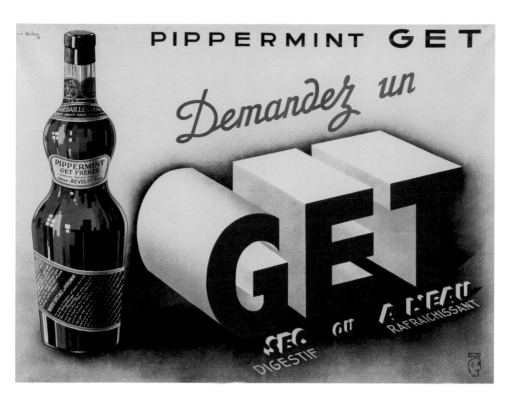

Pippermint Get advertisement, 1934.

## JUNGLE COCKTAIL
### *GIN VERSION*

*Jimmy Charters originally invented this drink as an equal-parts cocktail. We prefer this version.*

| | |
|---|---|
| *London dry gin* | 40 ML \| 1 ⅓ OZ |
| *French vermouth* | 20 ML \| ⅔ OZ |
| *Sherry* | 20 ML \| ⅔ OZ |

Stir the ingredients in a shaker tin over ice for fifteen seconds. Strain and serve in a chilled aperitif glass.

## JUNGLE COCKTAIL
### *MARTINI VERSION*

| | |
|---|---|
| *London dry gin* | 25 ML \| ⅞ OZ |
| *French vermouth* | 25 ML \| ⅞ OZ |
| *Sherry* | 10 ML \| ⅓ OZ |

Stir the ingredients in a shaker tin over ice for twenty seconds. Strain and serve in a small chilled coupe.

## KOZACK

*This Champagne cocktail was sure to be a hit during the fleeting months of summer along the Côte d'Azur. The mint liqueur was named after Jean and Pierre Get, who marketed it at the end of the nineteenth century under the name Pippermint.*

| | |
|---|---|
| *Yellow Chartreuse* | 20 ML \| ⅔ OZ |
| *Pippermint Get* | 20 ML \| ⅔ OZ |
| *Champagne for topping* | 90 ML \| 3 OZ |

Stir the chartreuse and Get in a champagne flute and top with Champagne.

## LEGION

*This cocktail's bitter taste comes from Luigi Palma's homeland. The name comes from his time in the French Foreign Legion.*

| | |
|---|---|
| *Italian vermouth* | 40 ML \| 1 ⅓ OZ |
| *Cognac* | 20 ML \| ⅔ OZ |
| *Cointreau* | 15 ML \| ½ OZ |
| *Fernet-Branca* | 2.5 ML \| ⅛ OZ |
| *Orange wedge* | |

Stir the ingredients in a shaker tin over ice for fifteen seconds. Strain and serve in a chilled aperitif glass. Squeeze orange wedge and garnish.

Pippermint Get advertisement, 1935.

## LUCIEN GAUDIN

*Four-time Olympic gold medalist between 1924 and 1928 and a team silver medalist, Lucien Gaudin was the top French fencer in the early twentieth century. Wielding sword and foil, he was a fixture of Paris high society but decided to leave the city in 1934.*

| | |
|---:|:---|
| *London dry gin* | 40 ML \| 1 ⅓ OZ |
| *French vermouth* | 15 ML \| ½ OZ |
| *Cointreau* | 15 ML \| ½ OZ |
| *Campari* | 15 ML \| ½ OZ |
| *Orange twist* | |

Stir the ingredients in a shaker tin over ice for fifteen seconds. Strain and serve in a chilled aperitif glass. Squeeze orange twist and garnish.

## MANHATTAN

*Once again a classic.*

| | |
|---:|:---|
| *Bourbon* | 40 ML \| 1 ⅓ OZ |
| *Italian vermouth* | 20 ML \| ⅔ OZ |
| *Angostura bitters* | 2 DASHES |

Stir the ingredients in a shaker tin over ice for fifteen seconds. Strain and serve in a chilled aperitif glass.

## MARNIER SPECIAL

*Bob's contribution to* La Coupole *magazine, which is reminiscent of Frank Meier's Olympic cocktail.*

| | |
|---|---|
| London dry gin | 50 ML \| 1 ¾ OZ |
| Grand Marnier | 20 ML \| ⅔ OZ |
| Orange juice | 20 ML \| ⅔ OZ |
| Orange twist | |

Combine the ingredients in a shaker over ice and shake for ten seconds. Double strain and serve in a chilled glass. Add a twist and garnish.

81

## (DRY) MARTINI

*For many years, the martini was prepared with equal parts gin and vermouth. The first mention of a dry martini appeared in the 1904 edition of Frank Newman's book* American Bar.

| | |
|---|---|
| London dry gin | 30 ML \| 1 OZ |
| French vermouth | 30 ML \| 1 OZ |
| Lemon twist or olive | |

Mix the ingredients in a shaker over ice for twenty seconds. Strain and serve in an aperitif glass. Garnish.

## MASTER JACK

*Promotional cocktail modeled after the Byrrh-Cassis recipe. The Master Jack served as an advertising campaign at the end of the 1930s, its theme being new ways to enjoy Byrrh. The recipe could also be found in Jean Lupoiu's cocktail book.*

| | |
|---|---|
| *Byrrh* | 50 ML \| 1 ¾ OZ |
| *Grand Marnier* | 10 ML \| ⅓ OZ |

Stir the ingredients in a shaker tin over ice for fifteen seconds. Strain and serve in a chilled aperitif glass.

82

## MONKEY'S GLAND

*Harry MacElhone's invention refers to Dr. Serge Vornoff's technique of grafting animal tissue onto men. The procedure was trendy during the 1920s and '30s. By grafting on a bit of monkey testicle tissue, patients purportedly became more virile.*

| | |
|---|---|
| *London dry gin* | 40 ML \| 1 ⅓ OZ |
| *Orange juice* | 40 ML \| 1 ⅓ OZ |
| *Grenadine* | 5 ML \| ⅙ OZ |
| *Absinthe* | 2.5 ML \| ⅛ OZ |

Combine the ingredients in a shaker over ice and shake for ten seconds. Double strain and serve in a chilled aperitif glass.

# OLYMPIC

*Another classic with orange juice, this one invented by Frank Meier.*

| | |
|---|---|
| *Cognac* | 50 ML \| 1 ¾ OZ |
| *Cointreau* | 20 ML \| ⅔ OZ |
| *Orange juice* | 20 ML \| ⅔ OZ |
| *Orange twist* | |

Combine the ingredients in a shaker over ice and shake for ten seconds. Double strain and serve in a chilled aperitif glass. Add twist and garnish.

# PACIFIC

*Charles at Harry's Bar in Le Touquet-Paris-Plage invented this one.*

| | |
|---|---|
| *London dry gin* | 40 ML \| 1 ⅓ OZ |
| *Cointreau* | 20 ML \| ⅔ OZ |
| *Cherry liqueur* | 20 ML \| ⅔ OZ |
| *Orange twist* | |

Stir the ingredients in a shaker tin over ice for fifteen seconds. Strain and serve in a small chilled glass. Squeeze orange twist and garnish.

Advertisement for Le Touquet Paris-Plage, 1927.

*Your Continental Holiday,* poster by Pieter Irvin Brown, 1932.

# PARIS

*Raquel Meller, "La Violetera", gives us her version of the City of Lights.*

| | |
|---|---|
| *London dry gin* | 40 ML \| 1 ⅓ OZ |
| *Grand Marnier* | 15 ML \| ½ OZ |
| *Cherry liqueur* | 15 ML \| ½ OZ |
| *Lemon juice* | 15 ML \| ½ OZ |

Stir the ingredients in a shaker tin over ice for fifteen seconds. Strain and serve in a chilled aperitif glass.

# PERROQUET APERITIF

*This cocktail has a double dose of vermouth and is typical of the era's aperitifs. Invented by Jean Lupoiu when he officiated over the Bar du Perroquet in Saigon.*

| | |
|---|---|
| *London dry gin* | 40 ML \| 1 ⅓ OZ |
| *French vermouth* | 20 ML \| ⅔ OZ |
| *Italian vermouth* | 20 ML \| ⅔ OZ |
| *Crème de cassis* | 5 ML \| ⅙ OZ |
| *Sparkling water* | |

Stir the ingredients in a shaker tin over ice for fifteen seconds. Strain and serve in a chilled aperitif glass. Top with sparkling water.

## PLAZA ATHÉNÉE

| London dry gin | 50 ML | 1 ¾ OZ |
| Cointreau | 20 ML | ⅔ OZ |
| Pineapple juice | 20 ML | ⅔ OZ |

Combine the ingredients in a shaker over ice and shake for ten seconds. Double strain and serve in a chilled aperitif glass.

## REGRETS INFINIS

*"I don't have any cocktail recipes. And I don't want my name associated with any of those concoctions. Because the doctor said I couldn't drink alcohol, I'm determined to deprive the rest of humanity of it. Still with the best intentions."*—Tristan Bernard

*VIE EN ROSE* <sup>P.99</sup>

90

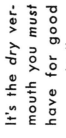

NOILLY PRAT
French Vermouth

It's the one that
is sponsored by
the House of
SCHENLEY.

★

NOILLY PRAT
French Vermouth

It's the genuine
imported ver-
mouth direct from
France

★

NOILLY PRAT
French Vermouth

It's the dry ver-
mouth you must
have for good
cocktails

★

To avoid disappointment, ask for it by its full name

NOILLY PRAT
French Vermouth

Noilly Prat advertisement
in a brochure for New York's Plymouth Theatre, 1934.

## RODOLPHE'S SPECIAL

*Just like Bob, Harry, Charlie, and Frank, Rodolphe had his own special!*

| | |
|---|---|
| *French vermouth* | 40 ML \| 1 ⅓ OZ |
| *Italian vermouth* | 40 ML \| 1 ⅓ OZ |
| *Grenadine* | 5 ML \| ⅙ OZ |
| *Absinthe* | 2.5 ML \| ⅛ OZ |

Stir the ingredients in a shaker tin over ice for fifteen seconds. Strain and serve in a chilled aperitif glass.

## ROSE

*Invented at the Chatam bar, this was the cocktail of the interwar period. Several versions existed.*

| | |
|---|---|
| *French vermouth* | 50 ML \| 1 ¾ OZ |
| *Kirsch* | 30 ML \| 1 OZ |
| *Cherry liqueur* | 20 ML \| ⅔ OZ |
| *Brandied cherry* | |

Stir the ingredients in a shaker tin over ice for fifteen seconds. Strain and serve in a chilled aperitif glass. Garnish.

# SEAPEA

*Frank Meier's ode to Cole Porter (C.P.), a friend and regular at the bar on rue Cambon. Absinthe replaces the Pernod here. Can be made as a fizz with or without egg white.*

| | |
|---:|:---|
| *Absinthe* | 30 ML \| 1 OZ |
| *Lemon juice* | 15 ML \| ½ OZ |
| *Simple syrup* | 15 ML \| ½ OZ |
| *Sparkling water* | |

Combine the ingredients in a shaker over ice and shake for fifteen seconds. Double strain and serve in a tall glass. Top with sparkling water.

92

# SIDE CAR

A CLASSIC EVER SINCE IT WAS INVENTED
IN LONDON IN THE EARLY 1920S.

*The version by Frank Meier, using pre-phylloxera Cognac, was the most expensive cocktail of the era.*

| | |
|---:|:---|
| *Cognac* | 40 ML \| 1 ⅓ OZ |
| *Cointreau* | 20 ML \| ⅔ OZ |
| *Lemon juice* | 20 ML \| ⅔ OZ |

Combine the ingredients in a shaker over ice and shake for fifteen seconds. Double strain and serve in a large chilled coupe.

## SIX CYLINDRES

*Citroën introduced its C6 model, the company's first six-cylinder car, at the 1928 Salon de l'Automobile. It would also be the name given to the bar on Avenue Wagram. Finally a cocktail that went 65 m.p.h.*

| | |
|---:|:---|
| *London dry gin* | 15 ML \| ½ OZ |
| *Dubonnet* | 15 ML \| ½ OZ |
| *French vermouth* | 15 ML \| ½ OZ |
| *Italian vermouth* | 15 ML \| ½ OZ |
| *Campari* | 15 ML \| ½ OZ |
| *Cherry liqueur* | 15 ML \| ½ OZ |

Stir the ingredients in a shaker tin over ice for fifteen seconds. Strain and serve in a chilled aperitif glass.

93

# SUZE

## APÉRITIF A LA GENTIANE

*POURQUOI donner la préférence à la SUZE parmi tous les apéritifs qui vous sollicitent?*

1° **PARCE QUE** la Suze est un apéritif à base de racine de gentiane fraîche ;

2° **PARCE QUE** les bienfaits de la racine de gentiane sont connus depuis les temps les plus reculés ;

3° **PARCE QUE** la racine de gentiane est recommandée par nombre de médecins comme tonique, pour stimuler l'appétit et ranimer les forces ;

4° **PARCE QUE** les montagnards ont toujours considéré la racine de gentiane comme une panacée universelle ;

5° **PARCE QUE** pour bien se porter et vivre longtemps il est indispensable d'en prendre un verre avant chaque repas.

*La SUZE se boit pure ou étendue d'eau. Si vous voulez en diminuer l'amertume, vous pouvez y ajouter du cassis ou du sirop de citron.*

94

Suze advertisement, 1930s.

## SUZE
### *CASSIS*

*Traditionally crème de cassis is added.*

| | |
|---:|---|
| *Suze* | 50 ML \| 1 ¾ OZ |
| *Cassis liqueur* | 10 ML \| ⅓ OZ |

Stir the ingredients in a shaker tin over ice for fifteen seconds.
Strain and serve in a chilled aperitif glass.

95

## SUZE
### *LEMON*

*Which can be replaced with lemon juice.*

| | |
|---:|---|
| *Suze* | 50 ML \| 1 ¾ OZ |
| *Lemon juice* | 15 ML \| ½ OZ |

Stir the ingredients in a shaker tin over ice for fifteen seconds.
Strain and serve in a chilled aperitif glass.

# THREE-MILE LIMIT

WHEN CUBA AND FRANCE MEET
OUTSIDE THEIR TERRITORIES.

*Harry MacElhone commented, "One of the effects of the Volstead
Act, people get busy when outside of the three miles."*

| | |
|---|---|
| *Cognac* | 40 ML \| 1 ⅓ OZ |
| *Rum* | 20 ML \| ⅔ OZ |
| *Lemon juice* | 10 ML \| ⅓ OZ |
| *Grenadine* | 5 ML \| ⅙ OZ |

Stir the ingredients in a shaker tin over ice for fifteen seconds.
Strain twice and serve in a small chilled cocktail glass.

# TUNNEL

*Invented by Robert "Bob" Card from Harry's New York Bar, the
ingredients are the same as in a Negroni, but Card added gin
and French vermouth in equal parts—hence a much drier drink.
This cocktail was awarded the top prize at the International
Championship of Professional Bartenders in Paris on February 2,
1929. The recipe would be published the following year by Harry
MacElhone in the new edition of his* ABC of Mixing Cocktails.

| | |
|---|---|
| *London dry gin* | 30 ML \| 1 OZ |
| *French vermouth* | 30 ML \| 1 OZ |
| *Campari* | 20 ML \| ⅔ OZ |
| *Italian vermouth* | 10 ML \| ⅓ OZ |
| *Grapefruit twist* | |

Stir the ingredients in a shaker tin over ice for fifteen seconds.
Strain and serve in a chilled aperitif glass. Squeeze grapefruit
twist and garnish.

## URODONAL'S COCKTAIL

*Dissolve a dose of Urodonal in ¾ water. Not very good!*

Cover for issue 7 of *Cocktails 39*,
journal of The Barman's Association of France, March 1939.

# BACCARAT

30<sup>bis</sup> RUE DE PARADIS.- PARIS X<sup>e</sup>

*ses verres à cocktails*

*ses shakers*

*ses mélangeurs*

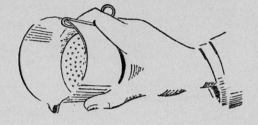

Advertisement for bar accessories, Baccarat, 1929.

## VIE EN ROSE

*Loosely inspired by one of the many versions of the Rose. Here, gin is replaced with tequila for a change!*

| | |
|---|---|
| *Tequila* | 40 ML \| 1 ⅓ OZ |
| *Kirsch* | 20 ML \| ⅔ OZ |
| *Lemon juice* | 15 ML \| ½ OZ |
| *Cherry liqueur* | 15 ML \| ½ OZ |
| *Brandied cherry* | |

Stir the ingredients in a shaker tin over ice for fifteen seconds. Strain and serve in a chilled aperitif glass. Garnish.

99

## WHISKEY SODA

*Like the name says: lots of whiskey and some soda.*

# WHITE LADY

*Invented by Harry MacElhone when he was at Circo's Club in London in 1919, this version of the classic consists mostly of Cointreau with crème de menthe and cognac. It would be another ten years before the definitive version would emerge, made with gin, Cointreau, and lemon juice as well as, if you wanted, egg white. Much better!*

| | |
|---|---|
| *London dry gin* | 40 ML \| 1 ⅓ OZ |
| *Cointreau* | 15 ML \| ½ OZ |
| *Simple syrup* | 10 ML \| ⅓ OZ |
| *Lemon juice* | 25 ML \| ⅞ OZ |
| *Egg white* | 20 ML \| ⅔ OZ |

Combine the ingredients in a shaker without ice. Shake vigorously for fifteen seconds. Add ice and shake again for fifteen seconds. Double strain and serve in a large chilled coupe.

# YELLOW COCKTAIL

*This cocktail got its name from the color of its two French liqueurs. Sipped along the Côte d'Azur, it was originally prepared with equal parts gin, Suze, and Chartreuse. Here it is made like a Last World, the cocktail invented in Detroit in 1925.*

| | |
|---|---|
| *London dry gin* | 20 ML \| ⅔ OZ |
| *Suze* | 20 ML \| ⅔ OZ |
| *Yellow Chartreuse* | 20 ML \| ⅔ OZ |
| *Lemon juice* | 20 ML \| ⅔ OZ |
| *Lemon twist* | |

Combine the ingredients in a shaker over ice and shake for thirty seconds. Double strain and serve in a chilled coupe. Squeeze lemon twist and garnish.

*YELLOW COCKTAIL* <sup>P.100</sup>

Advertisement for Chez Les Vikings restaurant,
from *Vikings d'hier et d'aujourd'hui*, 1930.

## 60° LATITUDE

THIS DRINK IS A VARIATION ON A ROSE.

*Ollé was inspired by the title of Mauric Bedel's novel* Jérôme 60° Latitude Nord, *which won the Prix Goncourt in 1927.*

| | |
|---:|:---|
| *London dry gin* | 40 ML \| 1 ⅓ OZ |
| *Kirsch* | 20 ML \| ⅔ OZ |
| *Cherry liqueur* | 20 ML \| ⅔ OZ |

Stir the ingredients in a shaker tin over ice for fifteen seconds. Strain and serve in a chilled aperitif glass.

## $ 1,000,000

*Twenty times more than Hemingway's short story, published in France in 1928.*

| | |
|---:|:---|
| *London dry gin* | 40 ML \| 1 ⅓ OZ |
| *French vermouth* | 20 ML \| ⅔ OZ |
| *Pineapple juice* | 25 ML \| ⅞ OZ |

Stir the ingredients in a shaker tin over ice for fifteen seconds. Strain and serve in a large chilled coupe.

Following spread: *GREEN HAT* P.74

# PARIS IS EVERY- WHERE

## THE COCKTAIL RADIATES IN AND OUT OF THE CITY

"Maigret walked up to La Coupole, noticed the entrance of the American bar where he entered. There were only five tables, all occupied. Most of the guests were perched on the high bar stools or standing around it."

Georges Simenon, *La tête d'un homme*, Paris, Fayard, 1931.

Young woman looking at the map for the North-South metro line,
Paris, around 1925.

# "DON'T WORRY...
# COME
# TO MONTPARNASSE"

### AT THE CROSSROADS OF THE WORLD

*"If Montparnasse is the center of the world, a table with a cocktail in the middle is the center of Montparnasse."*[1]

Modigliani was no more. Guillaume Apollinaire was buried to jeers of "Die Guillaume" (*sic*, Kaiser Wilhelm II, who had recently been deposed). Arthur Cravan had disappeared in the Gulf of Mexico. Legends were forged and the cocktail replaced the *café crème*.

The Closerie des Lilas, erected on the edge of the Quartier Latin, rekindled those Tuesday poetry gatherings but it was now transformed into a modern bar, and Paul Fort seemed somewhat lost alongside the American bar. The Closerie nevertheless retained a gentle tranquility, a far cry from the tumult of the Vavin junction. The effervescence that dominated there could be glimpsed because of all the signs lighting the boulevard. More than ever, the crossroads of the world was in the heart of Paris. Artists from every nation—Russians, Scandinavians, Japanese, and Americans (the international *café crème* scene)— were now joined by middle-class tourists and bystanders drawn in by those *Montparnos*, the bohemia Georges Michel-Georges described in his eponymous novel that made them party-hungry. Grillrooms, bars, cabarets, and dance halls were always full, and even though the painter Sam Granowsky, the cowboy of Montparnasse, got around by horse, there were some who missed the time when Picasso wasn't living in the Riviera. La Rotonde, a meeting spot for the Cubists thanks in part to its owner, the *Père* Libion, who put an end to obligatory refills, allowing customers to spend the entire day over a single cup is no longer what it was before the war. It had just taken over Le Parnasse, the small café at number 103 on the boulevard that

[1]− André Warnod, *Oscar Fabrès* Paris-Montparnasse, February 1929.
Oscar Fabrès was the illustrator of the book *Montparnasse Bar, Cafés, Dancings*, published in Paris in 1929, which included a text by André Salmon.

T'EN FAIS PAS ! VIENS

enquête
illustrée
sur le

montpar-
nasse
actuel

avec les réponses
de Mmes et Mrs
RACHILDE, DOLLY sis-
ters; H. DE régnier,
van Dongen, maurice
Dekobra, CHAMPLY,
cami, maurice ver-
ne, POL Rab, Payen,
J Delteil, r. WISNER,
E. fernand-DUBOIS,
DE FOUQUières, DOMINI-
QUE BONNAUD, m. GEOR-
GES-MICHEL, DUVERNOIS,
ZADkine, rappoport,
GRANowski, r. D ORGELES,
FRATELLINI, P. REBOUX.
préface, légendes, dessins
d'HENRI BROCA

À
MONTPARNASSE !"

Cover of the book *T'en fais pas! Viens à Montparnasse,*
*Enquête illustrée sur le Montparnasse actuel* by Henri Broca, Paris, 1928.

had been the first to exhibit the work of neighborhood artists
and now had dancing on its second floor.
Across from its outdoor seating area was the Dôme's. The owner
Paul Chambon and his progeny, the Vieux and the Nouveau Dôme.
Because the Dôme also underwent renovations and now included
an American bar and an outdoor seating area where international
elite would gather in the summer. Models met there and were
grouped by studio; and Americans, who were not to be seated
inside, by native city. Women outside wearing stockings drew
the attention of passersby, and soon that section of the boulevard
was called "Montparnasse Beach".
The Chambon family truly attended to its clientele. The new
menu at the Dôme was designed just for them. In addition
to cocktails (*MARTINI* [P.81], *ALEXANDER* [P.48], *SIDE CAR* [P.92], *ALASKA* [P.48],
and *SIX-CYLINDERS* [P.93], among others) there were also "American
specialties" like hot dogs, chile con carne, corn flakes,
and porridge. This last item, on par with the *café crème*, became
a must for party hangovers.

At 99, boulevard du Montparnasse, Le Select became the meeting
point for Anglo-Americans who had somewhat abandoned Le Dingo
(see page 112). Le Select got lively only at the end of the day,
for cocktails. The drink menu was almost the same as the Dôme's
(*MARTINI* [P.81], *ROSE* [P.91], *MANHATTAN* [P.80], and *ALEXANDER* [P.48],
among others) and there was a wide selection of liquors
and English beers. A cold buffet was available, but the specialty
of the house was Welsh rarebit, as good as in London, ready
to nourish revelers. Le Select was the first establishment
in Montparnasse to stay open all night. The night bar in
a neighborhood that never slept... and "coco" dealers wandered
the bathrooms.

### LE JOCKEY BELONGS TO HISTORY

At the corner of rue Campagne-Première and boulevard
du Montparnasse, at number 146, a sign lit up the most senior
member of the neighborhood's nightclubs, Le Jockey.
On the outside, painted murals of cowboys and indians, a draw for
Americans, gave the establishment a lonely saloon feel.
Inside, the walls and ceiling were covered in posters of many

colors glued every which way, along with a few signs; "We only lost
one customer... He died" is written in white letters.
The space was tiny and all of Montparnasse piled in. Near the
entrance was the wood bar where Andromache officiated;
patrons struggled to reach the dance floor, even though it was but
a few steps away. You had to weave your way through bodies that
were pushing more than dancing. Because of the cramped space,
the saxophone player perched on the piano. Kiki, soon to be
the appointed Queen of Montparnasse, was singing her staff-room
repertoire. Her eyebrows were dyed the same color as her dress,
a tease of a garment that surreptitiously revealed first her left
breast, then her right—and then, well, both. Her partner, La Môme
Chiffon, rivaled her performance, dancing on a table in front
of a delirious room, her dress tucked up. Soon it was impossible
to move around. Bodies were pressed up against one another.
It is said that one night a woman danced entirely naked and no one
noticed. The heat was stifling. The crowd was cosmopolitan,
and delighted. Artists, students, lots of foreigners—mostly
Americans but also South Americans, Spaniards, and high society
side-by-side. Outside, as proof of its success, a row of limousines
were parked along the sidewalk, waiting for their owners, which
prompted one of the chauffeurs to say, "The uglier it is, the more
they love it!"[2]
The American artist Hilaire Hiler conceived of the interior
decoration and ambiance. Partnered with the former jockey
Walter Miller when Le Jockey opened in November 1923,
Hiler was the one who brought in Kiki and drew on his network
of artist friends (Pascin, Foujita, and Kisling were among
the regulars). He managed the piano for a while, accompanied
by Les Copeland, who had previously appeared at the New York
Bar. Then Hawaiian banjos arrived to accompany the ivories.

Next, Hiler designed a new dance hall at 127, boulevard
du Montparnasse, a few hundred feet from the Jockey, called
La Jungle.[3] It was run by Henri Meunier-Colin, a former manager
at the Jockey, whence he stole Kiki for new gigs. The crowd
was snobbier, the orchestra and dancers were black; from 10 p.m.
to 2 a.m. the dancing was frenetic and the music was deafening.
Baby Esther could be spotted at the bar.
At La Jungle, the friendly bartender Jimmy Charters, who was there
since it opened, invented the eponymous cocktail. Ever since

[2] – André Warnod, *Fils de Montmartre* (Paris: Fayard, 1955).
[3] – In the early 1930s, Le Jockey would move to where La Jungle
once stood. Jockeys are forever!

112

Le Dingo, the former Irish boxer had found a way to build a loyal clientele. The Dingo, a bar and grillroom, was opened in October 1924 by the American Louis Wilson on rue Delambre, and it was *the* meeting place for Americans, especially writers, who also went to Le Select. There, during talk about Dempsey, Jimmy and Hemingway clicked.

For the time being, it was at the Falstaff that Jimmy, whose cocktails and heft were the secret attraction, practiced his art in a more serene manner and found his true regulars. At 42, rue du Montparnasse, one of the most luxurious bars opened, its simple and comfortable décor combining an English club and a French salon complemented by Baccarat glassware. On June 25, 1929, Jimmy faced record crowds: throngs invaded for the signing of Kiki's memoir. The book, with a preface by Foujita and photographs by Man Ray (Kiki was his lover and model), was published by Henri Broca and "looked like a Montparnasse studio", wrote Pierre Mac Orlan.

A bit farther down at 28, rue Vavin, the College Inn presented a discreet façade and was home to a cozy bar with soft rugs like a smoking room. The decoration was a mix of cards, dice, boxing gloves, and brightly colored paintings of horses and jockeys, roulette and dominos. It too was designed by Hiler.

*La Closerie des Lilas,* Paris, around 1900.
Anonymous photograph.

At the bar, Henri, who was also the manager, served whiskey
and cocktails that he called *Serpent de mer* or *Pointe d'amour*.
At the slightly subdued piano, Bud Sheppard, who was also at
the New York Bar for a few years, played until three in the morning.
It was at this same piano a few years later that Charles Trenet,
newly arrived from the south, would meet Johnny Hess.
Of course, for more dancing there was La Cigogne on rue Bréa,
a small venue. On the back wall was a painting of a jazz band,
and from the ceiling hung glass balls. Behind the bar was Raoul,
who had come from the Dingo and "helped us live to the beat
of the shaker", as Oscar Fabrès wrote on one of his caricatures.
Here too a diverse crowd was united by alcohol and rhythm.
They drank and they danced, because that's what it was all about.[4]

## JAZZ AND THE CHARLESTON

Dance halls, cabarets, and balls flourished because dancing
quenched a thirst for freedom; freedom of movement—because
bodies had been constrained by social codes for so long. The fox
trot, the shimmy, the Charleston: the body was being released,
sweating to new dances and rhythms from America.

113

It was General Pershing's troops who brought these new sounds
to France. The "Harlem Hellfighters" of the 369th U.S. Infantry
(integrated into the French army, this all-black regiment
would be awarded the Croix de Guerre for their valor in combat)
and their orchestra, led by Lieutenant James Reese Europe
(known to everyone else as Jim Europe), introduced jazz to France.
The orchestra, which included Noble Sissle, played throughout
the country (appearing on stage at the Théâtre des Champs-Élysées),
and their syncopation brought together the avant-garde, all of whom
were ardent fans. From Dada to the Surrealists, the sound
of jazz and its beats formed the perfect soundtrack for their artistic
investigations. Compositions by Darius Milhaud, Francis Poulenc,
and Erik Satie were influenced by American music. At the Bœuf
sur le Toit, the pianist Jean Wiener and Clément Doucet, joined
by Vance Lowry, were the first to propose a program that combined
classical music and American music. In the decade that followed,
Paris would welcome Duke Ellington and Louis Armstrong.

[4] – Jimmy Charters would recount his experiences and tell stories
about these Montparnasse establishments in the book *This Must Be the Place*,
which was published in 1934.

In the bars, there was a pianist or jazz band as well as variety shows, which were so popular at the time. From the Casino de Paris, where in 1917 Louis Mitchell and his Jazz Kings starred in the show *Laisse-les tomber*, which included celebrities Maurice Chevalier and Mistinguett (who would triumph in 1920 in the show *Paris qui jazz*, also at the Casino de Paris), to the Moulin-Rouge, where the Blackbirds led by Adelaide Hall (Florence Mills had just passed away) became a hit. Jazz was the music people danced to.

And the unrivaled queen of "Le Tumulte Noir" was the young Joséphine Baker.[5] In 1925, arriving in Le Havre from New York with a troupe of singers, dancers, and musicians, including Sidney Bechet, she could not have imagined that at age twenty she would be writing her memoirs.[6] The *Revue nègre*, the first entirely black variety show presented in Paris, was cheered for its latent eroticism. Then came triumphs as lead dancer at the Folies Bergères and the Casino de Paris, a European and worldwide tours, movies, and more. Baker was acclaimed and imitated. You could see her dance at Chez Joséphine, the cabaret she opened in Montmartre. She also danced every afternoon in the Jardin des Acacias, near the Arc de Triomphe.

In 1936 Chez Joséphine moved to the place where the cabaret Gerny's once stood, and where the year before, a singer named "la Môme Piaf" had made her debut.

Advertisement for the cabaret
"Chez Joséphine Baker", 1929.

[5] — Florence Mills, Adelaide Hall, and Joséphine Baker all starred on Broadway in the musical *Shuffle Along*, written by Noble Sissle and Eubie Blake.
[6] — Joséphine Baker, *Les mémoires de Joséphine Baker*, collected by Marcel Sauvage (Paris: Éditions Kra, 1927).

*Casino de Paris, La Joie de Paris, Joséphine Baker.*
Illustrated poster, 1932.

## VIKINGS YESTERDAY AND TODAY

Montparnasse wasn't just an "American colony"—it was also a "Scandinavian colony", and its embassy was on rue Vavin. Leather banquettes, framed fjord landscapes, waitresses with steel-blue eyes, the Vikings restaurant had every Nordic specialty on its menu. The former chef to the royal court of Norway served anchovies, marinated herring, black soup, reindeer filets, snow hen cookies, and local cheeses. And it all came with Bourgogne wines. Dining was accompanied by music; Mary Ditrix from the Folies Bergères sang her new repertoire. The Vikings was so successful that a second restaurant was opened on the Champs-Élysées, easily recognized by the masted longship atop its entrance.

A Scandinavian tavern, as the owners liked to call it, opened next door on rue Vavin, at number 31. At the Vikings, which opened in August 1926, there was an elegant bar for a sophisticated and demanding clientele. Indeed, the wood, the small leather-lined boxes, and the historical paintings gave it a cozy atmosphere, like a Norwegian inn. Seated at one of the stools before dinner you could snack on one of some fifty different sandwiches served on rye bread; these *smørrebrød* with smoked fish or cold cuts were the specialty of the house. They could even be delivered and were all the rage at social gatherings.
But above all, there was Ollé at the bar.

Ollé was one of the stars of Montparnasse, on par with the Falstaff's Jimmy and Henri at the College Inn. The bartender with the golden hair and golden heart would serve you all the specialties of the house, from local beers like Tuborg to Nordic aquavits and Swedish punch. But Ollé was most famous for his cocktails, his smooth and strong *ALEXANDER* [P.48] and one of his own concoctions, the *60° LATITUDE* [P.103]. Was it a wink to Maurice Bedel's novel that lightly dented the image of Scandinavian customs? At the Viking, you didn't joke about that. Austerity reigned. This wasn't an establishment for lonely men or tarts. Unaccompanied women were not allowed. Unless they knew you, for example the milliner Alice Karine, a neighbor and countrywoman, or the young Lola, who only drank the *BACARDI* [P.49]. So, "honest" women came in droves and knew they would be treated well. That earned the boss

Chez les Vikings at night, 1930.

of the establishment the nickname "Maquereau de Vavin" (the pimp of rue Vavin).
All that had no effect on Ollé, who knew how to capitalize on his fame. He also appeared on the cover of *T'en fais pas! Viens à Montparnasse* (Don't worry, come to Montparnasse), a small book published by Henri Broca in 1928.[7] The illustrated story of then-present-day Montparnasse included a series of interviews with all the celebrities who loomed large in the public eye. It was sold at the Vikings. They, too, published a small promotional book, *Vikings d'hier et d'aujourd'hui*.
"To spend a few moment at the Vikings bar is to travel, not in a chair but on a stool, through richly alluring tastes."[8]

## LA COUPOLE

*"La Coupole is the Universe, the United States of the World."*[9]

La Coupole opened on the evening of December 20, 1927, in the presence of 2,500 guests and as many bottles of Champagne. The police were called the following morning to remove the last recalcitrant party animals (including Louis Aragon, who a few months later would meet his wife-to-be, Elsa Triolet, there). Only then could the establishment finally close.

Ernest Fraux and René Lafon, brothers-in-law, had managed Le Dôme for a few years. Once thanked and dismissed with severance, they were able to rent the former coal yard they spotted at 102, boulevard du Montparnasse. Construction began in 1927. It would be the largest establishment in Montparnasse; a year after opening, La Coupole employed more than four hundred people and would shape the image of Paris.
La Coupole—the name refers to the architecture of its neighbors, Le Dôme and La Rotonde—had a ground-floor brasserie that could serve 450 guests, some at clothed tables. The twenty-four pillars that supported the structure were soon decorated by bohemian neighbors. On the second floor was a luxurious outdoor restaurant, La Pergola. It opened in May and was soon

118

[7] – Henri Broca loved Montparnasse, and Kiki too, and published the magazine *Paris-Montparnasse*, which came out in 1929. An art and literary magazine, it also printed all the neighborhood "news".
[8] – Paul Reboux, ed., *Vikings d'hier et d'aujourd'hui* (Paris: Les Vikings, 1930).
[9] – *Paris-Soir*, March 18, 1930

topped by a terrace on which artists would play pétanque.
Finally, a glass cupola covered the restaurant. And La Coupole,
it was a huge terrace with seven rows of pedestal tables thronged
by peanut vendors. During that period, construction continued
in the basement, where less than a year later a dance hall opened,
featuring two orchestras.

On the left side of the establishment, through a separate entrance
that led to the brasserie, one reached the American bar,
which was decorated by those who had just renovated La Closerie
des Lilas. Long and relatively narrow, the bar was separated from
the brasserie by a wall; in front of the wall were a bench, a few
tables, and chairs. A new shaker star, Bob Lodewyck, reigned there.
In 1931 Lodewyck was immortalized by Georges Simenon
in *La tête d'un homme*, a story about detective Maigret. In it,
the commissioner, who was not as familiar with cocktails as was
his writer, asks for a *MANHATTAN* [P.80], echoing the order
of a customer nearby. Lodewyck, who had learned the ropes
on transatlantic liners, was a stylish fellow, polished, always smiling
and discreet. "From behind his counter, he presided over all
the intimate events of Montparnasse", recounted André Warnod
in his 1951 memoir, *Fils de Montmartre*. Warnod continued, "He knew
everything, he saw everything and said nothing." More than
an anonymous witness, Lodewyck was also the sometimes confidant
of his colorful clientele as well as a helping hand to the most
destitute. His regulars were of course Kiki, Madeleine Anspach,
and Youki, Foujita's wife; Robert Desnos was also there but
had not yet declared his love for her. Moïse Kisling and Jules Pascin
kept a tab open for their friends. Roger Vitrac wrote his plays there,
and Antonin Arthaud occasionally stopped in.

The establishment published a little magazine in 1928, *Sous la
Coupole*. Lodewyck contributed a few cocktail recipes that were
popular—the *MARNIER-SPÉCIAL* [P.81], the *COUPOLE-COCKTAILS* [P.66],
and the *P.F.K.* The magazine would have only one issue and
the dance hall would close for good in 1939.

119

La Coupole, Paris, 1930s.
Anonymous photograph.

Interior of La Coupole.

# THE OTHER
# BANK

## THE CHAMPS-ÉLYSÉES

If you didn't feel like going to Montparnasse but instead wanted
to stroll along the Avenue des Champs-Élysées, at the corner
of the rue de Berri was Le Select, its Right Bank counterpart.
There you could sit outside on the terrace with a *café liégeois*
or order a cocktail. A cold buffet was available at any hour,
and you could find every Montparnasse specialty, from Welsh
rarebit and its pale ale to club sandwiches.

Across the way was the Bar du Berry, its comfortable armchairs
and decoration reminiscent of a private estate. Up the street you'd
pass the offices of the *New York Herald Tribune*, across from
the Hôtel California. The hotel's bar, frequented by journalists,
was managed by Georges, who, after learning the trade in London,
perfected his skills at the Criterion-Fouquet's.
Farther down was the Bar Guarani, at 13, rue d'Artois, run by Léon
Ferrari. Having worked at the casinos in Nice and Cannes
and at the Hôtel Claridge, Ferrari turned the establishment into
a high-end bar. The Guarani was *the* meeting spot for South
Americans because it was also the first bar-restaurant of its kind.
On the menu were empanadas, mondongo soup, and, on weekends,
*cordero al asador.*

But you might head up the avenue instead, toward number 9,
rue Washington. That establishment opened in 1924 and was
named after Rodolphe and Pico. It was then a bar-restaurant with
an orchestra that quickly became popular. Pico took care
of the restaurant while Rodolphe managed the bar, whose nickname
was "Petit Maxim's". Rodolphe had started as a junior chef
at the Savoy's restaurant in London and then completed his training
in Paris's great hotels. In 1931, after Pico left, the establishment
changed its name to Casita. All in wood, with a French-style

ceiling and paned facade, the bar and dining area filled the entire space like a tavern. Seated in a sculpted booth, guests could order one of the house cocktails, *RODOLPHE'S SPÉCIAL* [P.91].

If the traditional or rustic was not your thing, then you went to rue Poncelet. Aboard the Pingouin, at number 16, was the most atypical cabaret in Paris. The owner, Eugène-Georges Picard, known as Watson, was a former music-hall performer whose songs were recorded by both Columbia and Gramophone. He'd be waiting for you, donned in an admiral's uniform; at the entrance was written "first class dining room", because his cabaret resembled the inside of a steamship. Thus the dining room had a rudder, the red and green lights of a navigation system, and portholes with views onto the street. It also had a small orchestra, an American bar, and waitresses dressed as sailors. The place was packed. On the dance floor Watson sang a little song. Nightly entertainment included Asian dances, whirling dervishes, and "exotic celebrations". Sometimes around midnight, Watson and his sailors would bring mattresses onto the dance floor. It was time for the most anticipated event, girl fighting. Four young women in bathing suits would then face off in front of a wild audience.
But if two-bit exoticism was not your strong point and you wanted something more chic, well, then, the place to go was rue Penthièvre.

125

### JEAN COCKTAIL

Jean Cocteau's *Le Bœuf sur le Toit* was, firstly, music inspired by a Brazilian melody; composed by Darius Milhaud, it was meant to accompany the projection of a silent movie starring Charlie Chaplin. The surrealist ballet it became—known as *The Ox on the Roof: The Nothing Doing Bar* in English—featured an American bar as the set and cardboard masks made by artist Raoul Dufy, in which the Fratellini brothers moved about to the cinematographic tango in slow pantomime. Jean Cocteau's farce, "an American farce created by a Parisian who had never been to America"[1], was performed for the first time at the Comédie des Champs-Élysées on February 21, 1920. The performance caused quite a stir. Poor France! cried some, while others applauded wildly. It came to blows, as usual.

[1]—Maurice Sachs, *Au temps du Bœuf sur le Toit*
(Paris: La Nouvelle Revue Critique, 1939).

Le Bœuf sur le Toit was also a little bar, entirely covered in tiles, on rue Duphot, where a big guy from Charleville named Louis Moyses imported delicious foie gras from Alsace. Jean Wiener played piano there. Milhaud, who knew Wiener from their Conservatory days, talked him up to Jean Cocteau, who was proud of two things: knowing how to draw and playing jazz. Cocteau got Stravinsky to lend him a set of drums and practiced every night. The *samedistes* first, then friends.[2] Soon there wasn't a free seat in the house and they had to consider expanding.

Then Louis Moyses visited Cocteau to introduce his project to him. Legend has it that their friendship was born around a portrait of Arthur Rimbaud—Cocteau was amazed that a café owner had recognized the poet in the picture. It turns out that Moyses's mother was at Rimbaud's wake in Charleville. Under Cocteau's patronage, and taking the name of his ballet, Le Bœuf sur le Toit opened at 28, rue Boissy d'Anglas in December 1921. It was a large square room with a sign painted by Jean Hugo. Photographs by Man Ray hung on the walls; there was a black varnished bar and in the back was Jean Wiener joined by Clément Doucet, who could play piano until two in the morning all while chatting with friends or reading a detective novel. Affable Moyses welcomed guests personally and found a place for everyone. It was a high-end club, and the entire avant-garde was there— Radiguet and Max Jacob, Picasso and Tzara, André Gide and Rubinstein, Simenon and Chanel, alongside the Ballets Russes audience. You'd find Marcel Duchamp, *Unconcerned but not indifferent*, under *The Cacodylic Eye* of his friend Francis Picabia, who decorated the bar wall. The only person missing was Marcel Proust, who lamented that his health prevented him from going to the movies and to the Bœuf sur le Toit. Between the tables, they danced the shimmy, inebriated with art and alcohol.

After first being expropriated (illegal lease) and then forced to move a second time, the spot for a *WHISKEY SODA* [P.99] reopened at 26, rue Penthièvre in 1928. The bare walls were sprinkled with gold, and huge mirrors in the four corners created the illusion of infinity. Star lights hung from the ceiling. A portrait of Cocteau and the bar, forever busy with "les messieurs". Maurice, who learned the trade in the United States, still served the signature cocktail *LE BŒUF SUR LE TOIT* [P.54] as well as a new

---

[2] – Gathering around Jean Cocteau and Erik Satie, the art avant-garde began meeting for dinners on Saturdays (hence the name *samedistes*) at both places during the war.

Le Bœuf sur le Toit, drawing, 1926.

Postcards of the establishments Rodolphe & Pico and Cintra-Paris.

invention, the *CÔTE D'ÉMERAUDE* [P.65], to the most sophisticated international clientele.
Moyses, thriving, opened Le Grand Écart and Les Enfants Terribles, still under the aegis of Cocteau. From then on, gossips no longer called him Jean Cocktail but Jean Bar.

## MADELEINE AND OPÉRA

When it was time for an aperitif and you'd rather have a port than a cocktail, you had to go to 6, Square de l'Opéra, where Bar Cintra was located. It was the first tasting bar in Paris to represent the port brand; similar spots already existed in London and Amsterdam. Cintra's stated goal was to make its ports known through specialized establishments where you could taste the entire line under the best conditions. You could sit atop one of the stools around the empty barrels used as tables, or at the bar, where you'd find those same barrels with the name of their vintage. There was also a full selection of sherries and Spanish wines. Of course a sandwich buffet was available with more than ninety offerings (much more than certain establishments in Montparnasse). French and Italian charcuterie, salmon and caviar—the only difficulty was choosing. The venue was so successful that a second location opened in Paris, on the rue de Montmartre, as well as locations in Marseille, Lyon, and Nice.

On the Boulevard de la Madeleine you could make a stop in front of the Hôtel de Paris and go to the Viel bar. The clientele consisted mostly of businessmen, and Robert, who used to be at the Chatam, seemed not to have a hard time convincing the men that after work, it was cocktail time!
On the other side of the Madeleine, on the Boulevard Malesherbes, you might stop at number 4. Formerly the Café de la Poste, Le Forum opened right after World War I. In the 1920s, it was decorated by the artist Adolphe Léon Willette (one of the painters who contributed to the famous Montmartre cabaret, Le Chat Noir) and quickly became one of the most elegant bars in the capital. In 1931 Le Forum would be taken over by Antoine Biolatto, an Italian immigrant from the Piedmont region. Antoine was working in a café on the Place de la Madeleine when he learned that Le Forum was for sale; since he did not have enough money

129

to purchase it, his clients, the most loyal of their kind, lent him
the necessary amount.
In the meantime, you could enter via the left side entrance,
the revolving door, and order a *$1,000,000* [P.103] or a *FORUM
COCKTAIL* [P.69] from among the specialties.

On the rue Édouard VII, which wasn't far, was Les Jardins d'Elmano
and the latest fashionable cabaret. Formerly named Luigi Elmano,
the cabaret and its *American bar for Americans* were opened
by an Italian named Luigi Palma in 1919. At the time, you could
drink his invention, the *LEGION* [P.78]. Next he opened Luigi's,
a bar near the Champs-Élysées. Too bad you didn't stop in. As for
the Jardins d'Elmano, they still served the best cocktails in Paris.
Well, that's what they claimed anyway.

## SANK ROO DOE NOO

To visit the United States, you no longer needed to cross
the Atlantic. You could simply go to 5, rue Daunou, where you
would be welcomed not by an American but by a Scotsman.
Born in Dundee in 1890, Harry MacElhone began his career
in New York and then headed off to the casinos of the Riviera
and Aix-les-Bains before World War I; after the war, it was
on to London. Working first at the Savoy, MacElhone became
the head bartender at Ciro's. It was during this period that he wrote
the short booklet meant to fit perfectly in a coat pocket—Harry's
*ABC of Mixing Cocktails*. It has since become a classic. Upon
his return to France, in 1923 Harry became the owner of the New
York Bar, to which he added his first name.

Harry's New York Bar is still a real American bar. It is decorated
all in wood; inside you will find a library where the best spirits
are displayed and whose walls are decorated with Sem cartoons
as well as newspaper clippings about the owner. Shuffling behind
the counter among the other Anglophone waiters, was Robert
"Bob" Card, who had returned from the Hotel Alexandria
in Los Angeles. Boxing enthusiasts joined horseracing devotees.
Harry was a fan, and his patrons could buy tickets for the fights
at the Salle Pleyel and Salle Wagram. (In fact, there hung at the bar
a huge pair of gloves that Primo Carnera left as a souvenir after

130

For years the Anglo-American colony of Paris throught itself unimportant — useless — and not even funny.

And then **The Boulevardier** came along and found out - they **are** funny. They're terribly funny - they're priceless.

They still dont know it, but **The Boulevardier** does.

Read

# THE BOULEVARDIER

published monthly in Paris by Erskine Gwynne, 65-67, av. des Champs-Élysées.

Ask for it on the stands. Subscription rates are sixty francs a year for France, and seventy-five for elsewhere.

— 52 —

stopping in.) But the establishment was above all the territory of Americans on the Right Bank, a place where they made light of the Eighteenth Amendment. Another bartender, "Chips", invented the *THREE MILE LIMIT* [P.96] cocktail, and Harry created the Volstead Act (with rye whiskey and Swedish punch) as a way to thank Andrew Volstead for sending so many customers his way. Expats and tourists crowded in to Harry's bar as well. American journalists and men of letters turned the place into their headquarters, with Arthur Moss and Erskine Gwynne at the fore. To celebrate their newly founded magazine, Gwynne created the publication's eponymous cocktail *THE BOULEVARDIER* [P.59], which was rather successful.

It was for his American clientele that Harry phonetically translated the bar's address into English. "Sank roo doe noo" was all you needed to say to the taxi driver to make sure you got to the right place. It was also for those "expats" and passing tourists that Harry organized the straw vote during the American presidential elections. It was a straw poll because expats weren't allowed to vote; instead, they were given the opportunity to gather together and prove "loyalty" to their country through a parallel voting event.

131

Advertisement for the journal *The Boulevardier*, 1930.

Invited to drop a ballot in Harry's official box, they cast their votes, which would then be counted on the day before the results of the real U.S. presidential election. On that night, everyone gathered around the radio waiting to compare results, never forgetting of course to drink to each new announcement.
It was also in 1924 that Harry founded the International Bar Flies (IBF), an association of "bar pillars", the top one being Harry's. Harry presented the list of members and its international ramifications in the book *Barflies and Cocktails*, which he published in 1927. It was under the auspices of the association that he created a beer-drinking contest. The rules were relatively simple: drink two liters of beer in the least amount of time. The record was eleven seconds, achieved in 1932.

While waiting for the next contest, you could drink the MONKEY'S GLAND P.82, a wink to the experiments of Doctor Voronoff, the fashionable French surgeon. Voronoff proposed to graft monkey tissue onto humans as a way to revive their youth and ardor. (Here's hoping the cocktail has the same effect.)

## OLD
## MONTMARTRE

There were the heights of Montmartre, *la butte*, a kind of country within a country, where the memory of the *rapins*, art students distinguished by their berets and large cloaks, lived on. And then there were the Montmartre lowlands, Pigalle, where debauchery reigned. Where tourists mingled with the underworld, the cabaret singer, and crime.

On the *butte*, the memory of Henri de Toulouse-Lautrec was still alive. Although he wanted to become a jockey, he became a painter of balls and brothels instead. In 1886 he drew *Gin Cocktail*, in which the barmaid behind a bar is serving men in top hats. That barmaid might be Sarah, an expert in cocktails and an English teacher who worked at the Moulin-Rouge. During his travels to London, Lautrec came to know about such drinks. He frequented the bars and when he wasn't at the Moulin de la Galette or sketching La Goulue dancing the cancan, he was hosting parties at his home, where American drinks were the guest of honor. Dressed in a white jacket, Lautrec invited the bartenders he knew—and there were many—to make cocktails he invented for his guests.
Alphonse Allais's shadow also lingered over the *butte*. Or was it Captain Cap's? The two were interchangeable. Allais would go from bar to bar writing his chronicles, crossing paths with Captain Cap, whose madcap adventures and love of drink he would transcribe. Allais knew those stories well because they were in fact his own. The cocktail recipes his character shared in his 1902 book *Le captain Cap: Ses aventures, ses idées, ses breuvages* were those served at the Criterion, where Allais was a regular.

But all that was yesterday. Now it was "Paris by Night"... the posters were tempting. And so buses filled with tourists traveled to the *butte* and discharged their cargo in front of a few cabarets where the Montmartre repertoire was sung. Then they headed down toward those in Pigalle, winding among the narrow streets and sidewalks so often described by Francis Carco,[1] where drugs and prostitutes pounded the pavement.

Pigalle was a place for pleasure, licit and not, and it was the neighborhood of cabarets of varying elegance. There was Chez Joséphine on rue Fontaine, near the Place Blanche, where Joséphine Baker would arrive around one in the morning with streamers and party favors, inviting you to join her on stage for a dance. There was also the Grand Écart at 7, rue Fromentin, a tiny venue. The place offered no entertainment, but there was a dance floor and a jazz orchestra. The walls were soundproof because the Grand Écart had already faced eviction for disturbing the peace. (Neighbors had complained!) At number 5 on the same street was the Bistrot Russe. To note, Pigalle was a Little Russia. Ever since the first presentation of Serge Diaghilev's Ballets Russes at the Théâtre du Châtelet in 1909 (except during the war, the company would perform in Paris every year until Diaghilev's death, in 1920), the era was known as the "Russian Years". But from the palette of Bakst's sets and costumes, Stravinsky's music, and Nijinsky's choreography, the trends retained only the exoticism of a Slavic and tormented soul, an exoticism that became a caricature in the figure of the "Russian taxi driver". Following successive waves of immigration after the 1917 revolution and civil war, the "Russian taxi driver", who crossed the streets of Paris, was an officer of the czar's army who now had to be a chauffeur to survive. Or an impoverished nobleman was now a café waiter, an admiral of the imperial fleet who now worked as a doorman.[2] It was this stereotype that all Pigalle cabarets would exploit. From the Château Caucasien to the Shéhérazde, the recipe was the same: Cossacks, gypsy singers, and dancers.[3] You would dance and eat (caviar, smoked fish, pickles) and you would drink vodka. Outside the Eastern European establishments and community, however, vodka had limited popularity. Vladimir Smirnov, ousted from Russia, Frenchified his name by spelling it Smirnoff, but vodka still wasn't a hit. The French thought it didn't taste like much.

134

[1] – Since his first novel *Jésus-la-Caille*, published in 1914,
Francis Carco was the "scene's" writer.
[2] – Joseph Kessel, *Nuits de princes* (Paris: Les Éditions de France, Paris, 1927).
[3] – Konstantin Kazansky, *Cabaret Russe* (Paris: O. Orban, 1978).

Advertisement for Pigall's cabaret, 1930s.

The Black Birds at the Moulin-Rouge, Paris. Postcard.

# FROM
# DEAUVILLE
# TO MONTE CARLO

"At the Miramar bar, come time for the daily dip, the English and South Americans, perched on high stools, drink cocktails and speak in loud voices. Two Frenchmen arrive and ask for two Pernods: *Well then!* says one of the Englishmen straightening up, *foreigners!*"[1]

It was not so long ago that swimming in the sea was for those suffering from rabies. Now seaside resorts looked like Paris. Paris was everywhere[2], so was New York, London and Buenos Aires. People had been swimming and covering their bodies in oil to tan ever since Gabrielle Chanel launched the trend. (Chanel had a boutique in Deauville and also in Biarritz, and Jean Patou opened swimsuit stores there. Patou was also the one who, after inventing sportswear, marketed the first suntan oil, Huile Chaldée, in 1927.) "Everywhere" meant on the beach but also in hotels, casinos, at the racetrack, polo grounds, and golf course... And everybody knows the cocktail is the sportsman's friend. The coast was no longer the privilege of monarchs, and the cocktail was no longer the privilege of Paris. The capital's bartenders headed south to do their season at seaside casinos. In 1928 Harry MacElhone opened his Harry's Bar at Touquet-Paris-Plage and managed the bar at the Deauville racecourse during the Grand Prix; Luigi Palma opened his that same year as well.

137

Deauville was the most popular of such resorts; it was also three hours away by train, the closest one to Paris. Le Casino was opened in 1912, then came the hotels Le Normandy and Le Royal, each the initiative of Eugène Cornuché, the happy proprietor of Maxim's.
At the Bar du Soleil at cocktail hour they drank the *ALFONSO* P.49, since his highness Alfonso XIII, king of Spain, had made it his custom to spend three weeks in Deauville every summer. Right nearby, the Crash bar opened in 1932. At the casino,

[1] – Paul Chantecaille, *Regard sur le passé* (Bordeaux: Feret et Fils, 1930).
[2] – Title from a *Comoedia magazine* column on the current state of summer resorts.

Fred Martin welcomed visitors between games of baccarat. The head bartender at the casino's bar served his own inventions, including the *DEMPSEY* [P.66] and the *SAINTE-URSULE*.

Americans rarely visited Biarritz on the Basque coast; rather, tourists hailed from England and South America, because of the proximity to Spain. That "queen of beaches" was historically where the aristocracy converged. The holiday spot of Napoléon III's wife, Empress Eugénie, the Hôtel du Palais was built where her home had once stood. Life in Biarritz involved a midday swim and gambling at the Bellevue casino, which had just opened. Games started at six o'clock in the evening and ended at six in the morning. Of course there were many galas and parties, for example one called "Aux Pieds de Pyrénées", for which Basque dancers and singers gathered at the Hôtel du Palais; then there was the *concours d'élégance* at the Hôtel Miramar. The other curiosity was the Basque bar, which would lend its name to a new style of American bar that later popped up in Paris, decorated like a typical Basque inn, with local crafts.

138

Basil Woon called the stretch between Nice and Monte Carlo the "Dollar Coast". From Nice, where reportedly more than ten thousand cocktails were consumed per day,[3] to the Café de Paris and its terrace nicknamed "the bask" (because you could sip your drink in the sun for hours), there was nothing more than a string of palaces, villas, casinos, and American bars. The fashionable cocktail along the coast was the *FIOUPE* [P.68], which was served in the most reputed establishments, including the New York Bar in Nice (member of the IBF), the Cannes casino bar where Fred Martin also officiated, and the casino and baccarat bars in Juan-les-Pins. This last coastal resort town owed much to Florence Gould. She was one of the first to spend the summer along the coast, breaking the custom of going only around September. And it was she who adopted pajamas for the beach. The custom became such a craze that Juan-les-Pins quickly became known as Pajamapolis.
Starting in 1936, newcomers invaded the beaches. The emergence of the Front Populaire and the institutionalization of paid vacations turned "society" beaches into family beaches. Quietly and with joy, they took in the sea and the sun... while looking at the Carlton.

[3] *Paris-Soir*, February 15, 1924.

Terrace of the American Bar, Les Planches, Deauville, 1925.

Juan-les-Pins beach, 1934.
Anonymous photograph.

# KINGS OF THE SHAKER

"They knew perfectly well that Serge Salvagno from the Sporting Club in Cannes was a student of the famous Nut from New York's Knickerbocker, which the illustrious Harry started, or practically, before the war, at the Plaza in New York as well... They knew their itineraries, followed their whereabouts, and believed they understood their style."

Raymond Queneau, *Les Enfants du Limon*, Paris, Gallimard, 1938.

*Moulin-Rouge, Paris qui tourne, Mistinguett.* Illustrated poster, 1928.

Cover of the book *Cocktails de Paris*, Demangel, Paris, 1929.

## COCKTAILS DE PARIS
## PRESENTED BY RIP AND ILLUSTRATED
## BY PAUL COLIN, 1929

At 5 p.m. on Saturday, February 2, 1929, a dense but particularly elegant crowd filled the sidewalk around 20, rue de Clichy. The Apollo (the theater founded in 1905 that was popular for music and had suffered a few recent setbacks) opened its doors for the First International Championship of Professional Bartenders. For thirty francs, guests could "taste the cocktails provided by all competitors", quenching both their curiosity and their thirst at each of the bars managed by the forty best bartenders in Paris. Because the jury consisted of the audience, each ticket also came with a ballot; it was the public who ranked competitors and named the best among them. And so, whether out of professional obligation or for pleasure, every drink had to be tried. In its edition of January 31, 1929, *L'Intransigeant* noted that "indispensable precautions have been taken, medical services are provided, and stretcher-bearers are on call!"

"Rarely able to complete the challenge, the drinkers, in order to avoid permanently soiling the theater's carpets, were quickly dispatched on stretchers to the sidewalk of rue de Clichy and there awaited their fate", wrote Paul Colin in his memoirs, *La croûte* (1957).
Honorable Mentions, Grand Prize, First Prize... no less than forty cocktails were offered to seasoned enthusiasts and novices alike.

The championship was organized by the Maison du Cocktail (apartment bars sold at 83, rue de la Boétie!), with the sponsorship of such big brands as Cointreau, Bénédictine, and Dubonnet (the acknowledged goal being the promotion of French products) and supported by *La Semaine à Paris.*
This last was the newspaper circulated by Paris's tourist office (published beginning in 1920 in a French edition; an English edition as well as a French-Spanish-American edition were added later). Inside this illustrated weekly, readers would find everything "to see, hear, and do in Paris". In its pages were listings and reviews

of every show, style and cuisine reports, literary and sports reviews, information about trains and boats, hotel and restaurant recommendations... A "practical" newspaper, the indispensable guide to discovering Paris, *La Semaine à Paris* promoted the championship by publishing the rules, offering coupons for tickets at a lower price, and printing portraits of participants and the results in its February editions.

The rules were simple: competitors paid a registration fee of 150 francs, submitted an envelope listing the liquors they needed (preferably ones produced by the brands at hand), and proposed a single cocktail recipe. They were then given access to a bar with all the necessary items to prepare it.

Who were the participants?
Among the shaker "aces" were Robert "Bob" Card (Bar No.19) from Harry's New York Bar, winner of one of the Grand Prizes for his *TUNNEL'S COCKTAIL* [P.96], and Robert Carme (Bar No.2) from Viel for his *BOULEVARDIER* [P.59] recipe. Honorable mentions were awarded to Charlie Rola from Cheval Pie for his *LUCIEN GAUDIN* [P.80] and Jimmy Charters and his *JUNGLE COCKTAIL* [P.76] from the bar La Jungle. Also Charles from Harry's Bar in Le Touquet for his *PACIFIC* [P.84] cocktail...

Thanks to the participation of the foremost bartenders and the most reputed establishments, the championship was an unprecedented success, despite the deplorable incident that cast a shadow on the end of the competition.

The management of the Apollo suddenly cut off electricity well before the designated hour, plunging the hall into total darkness. Police were quickly called in to conduct an evacuation, without motive or disruption reported by the organizers! What followed was broken glass, looting, and various accidents... Had not enough "indispensable precautions" been taken? The organizers intended to pursue legal options relating to the incident...

*Cocktails de Paris* was published in 1929, presented by Rip and illustrated by Paul Colin; the two knew each other well.
Rip was the pen name of Georges Gabriel Thenon, prince of the French revue; he entrusted Paul Colin with the set and costume design for almost all of his theatrical performances. Colin, a painter from Nancy, was already famous for his work with the Théâtre des Champs-Élysées. In 1925 Rolf de Maré,

# A SEMAINE À PARIS

journal illustré hebdomadaire paraissant le jeudi

## ce qui se verra, s'entendra, se fera à Paris

Du 25 janvier au 1er février 1929

## édition française

n° 348

journal du
syndicat d'initiative de paris

dans tous
les kiosques

*The Week in Paris,* journal of the Paris Tourism Office,
issue 348, January 25–February 1, 1929.

# PREMIER
# Championnat de Cocktail
## DES
## BARMEN PROFESSIONNELS

### LE 2 FÉVRIER
SOUS LE PATRONAGE

de

## LA SEMAINE A PARIS

à 17 heures.

# A L'APOLLO

## RUE DE CLICHY

Tous les cocktails préparés par les
### MEILLEURS BARMEN DE PARIS

Entrée : 30 fr. (toutes taxes comprises)

*Donnant droit à déguster les cocktails*
*de tous les concurrents*

Voir dans ce numéro et dans le numéro suivant tous les détails de
ce championnat. la notice biographique consacrée aux barmen ins-
crits. la liste des prix offerts aux barmen et aux assistants.

Les lecteurs de la « Semaine à Paris » seront admis moyennant la
somme de 20 francs (toutes taxes comprises). au lieu de 30 francs,
en découpant le billet à prix réduit publié dans ce numéro. billet de fa-
veur exclusivement réservé à nos lecteurs.

creator of the Ballets Suédois and director of the Théâtre
des Champs-Élysées at the time, along with art director André
Daven, hired Colin to create the posters and sets for their
performances. It was that same year, in the month of October,
that Colin enjoyed recognition for painting a poster and portrait
of a certain Joséphine Baker, the African-American entertainer
who ignited Charleston fever in Paris.
Paul Colin's fame reached its peak in 1927 with the publication
of *Le tumulte noir*, an homage to that "crazy dance" and to jazz
in the form of a portfolio of forty-four illustrations. Its preface
was written by none other than Rip.

*Cocktails de Paris* is a collection of recipes. Many among them came
from different competitions organized in 1928 and 1929, with
the most coming from the Apollo championship.
But alongside certain classics (*BRONX* [P.60], *GIN FIZZ* [P.70], *SIDE CAR* [P.92],
etc.) and recipes invented by shaker professionals, you'll find
recipes, sometimes approximate, from music hall stars, artists,
and celebrities from Paris high society. Such was the case with
Maud Loty and *Un Chien Qui Rapporte*, the title of the play
in which she performed in 1924; Raquel Meller, "La Violetera",
and her cocktail *PARIS* [P.87]; Abel Gance and *La Fin du Monde*,
the title of his forthcoming movie; the four-time Olympic gold
medalist in fencing, Lucien Gaudin, with *BIRIBI* [P.54], and created
the *CHARLIE PIE* [P.65] in homage to Charlie Rola, bartender
at the Cheval Pie, who had dedicated a cocktail in honor of Gaudin
at the forementioned First International Championship of
Professional Bartenders. Paul Colin himself created the
*BARBARESQUE* [P.53].
While Rip, with his usual witty eloquence, championed "alcohol
at home" and "boozing up with the family", in his preface
Maurice Des Ombiaux was invited to expound on the harmony
that must emanate from a cocktail, as in a marriage, more
than a harmonious mix. Des Ombiaux again emphasized
the parallels between the cocktail and good cuisine, the importance
of adapting the cocktail to France, and, like French gastronomy,
"of composing a pleasant drink in the manner in which a chef
achieves a good dish".[1]

Through its recipes, (even the wackiest ones, like *REGRETS
INFINIS* [P.88] or *URODONAL'S COCKTAIL* [P.97]) *Cocktails de Paris*

[1] — Maurice Des Ombiaux, *L'œil de Paris*, November 10, 1928.

# le 1er championnat

seules les grandes marques seront employées pour la préparation des cocktails du championnat

Max TAILLIEZ
commissaire général.
(Photo Arax.)

à l'apollo, 20, ■
15 ■

## il existe un art

Le cocktail est une boisson qui convient à notre temps de fièvre, de business à outrance. Mais, attention ! il y a cocktail et cocktail, et l'on ne parvient à en réussir un parfait qu'après de savantes études de dosages. Cette difficulté même n'ôte à l'orgueil humain la tentation de se surpasser, à lui et de confiance lui-même pour prier ses amis de déguster un cocktail de sa façon : un short-drink, un musqué-manhattan, un doux alexandra, voire un « rose » classique et bien équilibré. Personnellement, je considère qu'il y a un art dans la fabrication du cocktail, il n'est pas aisé d'en réussir un, hélas ! classique. Que de ratages y a-t-il ! Les maîtres du shaker et du tumbler fabriquent, eux, des cocktails qui sont de vrais

GORDON'S DRY GIN

COINTREAU

PERNOD FILS

AMAROS

IMPERIAL-COCKTAIL

ROMANO

COURVOISIER
« THE BRANDY OF NAPOLEON »

---

# international de cocktail

des
Barmen
professionnels

organisé sous le patronage
de
*la semaine à paris*

le samedi 2 février
de 17 à 19 heures

*rue de clichy*

le championnat
est organisé
avec
la participation
des
grandes marques

■

## du cocktail :

régals, tels que le « brandy crusties », confectionné par Harry, ou encore « l'alexandra », spécialité du bar des Vikings. Ce ne sont pas des cocktails, mais de véritables petits poèmes. D'ailleurs les professionnels ou amateurs ne procèdent pas que de la même manière, et j'en ai vu qui avaient une méthode vraiment personnelle ; ainsi, n'ai-je pas vu (et c'était récemment) un gentleman américain qui, muni des liqueurs nécessaires et d'un shaker, fit son dosage dans un gobelet à mélange, pour jeter ensuite tout le contenu dans le shaker ? Quelle erreur ! Il ne faut pas le faire ! L'art du cocktail ne réside pas seulement dans le dosage des liquides, mais dans la façon dont les alcools sont précipités dans la glace qui

CHERRY - ROCHER

MOET & CHANDON

BÉNÉDICTINE

DUBONNET

JOHNSTON COCKTAIL

CAMPARI

JOHNIE WALKER WHISKY

was a special account of a special decade, one that ended on "Black Thursday", October 24, 1929.

It is a snapshot of ten years of euphoria when the cocktail escorted the frenzy of the Roaring Twenties—part of every celebration, every show, every all-nighter and indulgence...

For a moment, it is now time to wish it good-bye...

"And as for the people of happy and prosperous times, we must undoubtedly bid them farewell."[2]

151

[2] – Maurice Sachs, *Au temps du Bœuf sur le Toit* (Paris, Grasset & Fasquelle, 1939).

Cover of the book *Cocktails* by Jean Lupoiu.
Les Œuvres Françaises, Paris 1938.

## COCKTAILS
## JEAN LUPOIU
## 1938

Four days, three hours, and five minutes.
Upon its arrival in New York, the "Giant of the Atlantic" was awarded the Blue Riband after completing its inaugural voyage.[1] Departing from Le Havre on May 29, 1935, the steamship known as the *Normandie* was celebrated by an entire city, which gathered to greet it well beyond port. After this triumphant welcome, which went on for over four days, there were dinners and galas before the return voyage to Le Havre, during which it would set a new speed record, exceeding its performance on the first leg of the trip. The *Normandie* was the French Line's jewel, the largest and most luxurious liner as well as the fastest, and it was the pride of France during the mid-1930s. A veritable "floating palace", the vessel was remarkable for its technical achievements and unforgettable for the splendor of its decor, "a floating exhibition of all the French decorative arts".[2] The apartments, suites, pool, smoking room, and grill rooms (with their never-dry bars) were the work of France's most famous craftsmen.
The stakes were high. Diplomatic and economic intentions were front-and-center. The stated goal was to tighten the relationship between the two countries during a time of crisis, but especially to satisfy an American clientele that had become increasingly demanding, and to lure them back to Paris, a city they had all but abandoned.[3]

Another "palace" was inaugurated in September 1936, the Hôtel Plaza Athénée in Paris. The inauguration, however, was really a reopening. After the recession endured by the hotel industry

153

---

[1] - The Blue Riband, symbolizing the fastest crossing of the Atlantic Ocean, was awarded upon calculation of the average speed between two fixed points, the Bishop Rock lighthouse and the Lightship Ambrose.

[2] - *Normandie: Chef-d'œuvre de la technique et de l'art française* [The *Normandie*: Masterpiece of French art and technique] (Paris: L'Illustration, 1935).

[3] - "L'État actuel du commerce Franco-Américain et du trafic transatlantique," in *France-Amérique*, monthly periodical of the Comité France-Amérique, September–October 1935.

following the stock market crash, and with increasingly few
travelers, the Plaza Athénée was unable to overcome massive
financial losses and had no choice but to declare bankruptcy.
The new buyer was François Dupré, who had just taken over
the Georges V. Dupré had never been in the hotel or restaurant
business. His business was horses (again!)—as the owner of the
Dupré stables, and his milieu was dominated by the racetrack—
and quite a few bars.
With the arrival of Dupré, a new world entered the Plaza Athénée.
In its previous life, it had been the hotel of the aristocracy
and its strict rules, including tea; now there was high society
and cocktails. But no clash occurred. In March 1939 the Plaza
Athénée proposed that the two worlds come together for "tea
and cocktail hour"!
The Plaza Athénée succeeded in protecting its patrons from social
conflicts, and for a while at least, kept the drums of war at bay.

The Relais Plaza opened at 21, Avenue Montaigne on December 30,
1936. Its art deco interior, inspired by the *Normandie*'s suites,
was the work of architect and designer Constant Lefranc.
To access the restaurant, one went through the bar. The same bar
that undoubtedly hailed the Relais's modernity.

In order to attract theatergoers to the nearby Théâtre des Champs-
Élysées, the Relais offered a quick after-show supper, served
directly on a covered plate. It also became a meeting place
for elegant women. Couturiers Paul Poiret, who was already settled
at the Rond-Point des Champs-Élysées, and Madeleine Vionnet,
who was at number 50 on Avenue Montaigne, lunched at the Relais
and were fond of the cocktails. (Around the same time, had not
Jean Patou set up a bar where ladies could savor an "American
drink" between presentations?)

A key figure in French cocktails during the interwar period was
Jean Lupoiu, who held the reins at the Relais Plaza bar.
Born in Romania in November 1898, Lupoiu began his bar career
in Bucharest when he was twenty-three; after a stint in Naples,
he arrived in Paris in 1924. Then it was in Saigon where he could
be found managing the Bar du Perroquet, next to the Continental
Palace Hôtel.
A widely known hotel in French Indochina during the colonial
period, the Bar du Perroquet opened in 1880; in 1926 it housed

A.M. Cassandre, *Normandie*, 1935.

the newly founded Official Tourist Bureau of Cochin China. A visit
to the bar was essential for all foreigners and Saigonese who, atop
stools or seated near the patio, could sip an *APÉRITIF PERROQUET* [P.87],
or a *BAISER D'AMOUR* [P.50] ...

During the quick two years he spent there, Lupoiu wrote a book
titled *370 recettes de cocktails*—370 cocktail recipes. An explicit title.

*Cocktails*, from 1938, is the second edition of that book. Clearly,
after ten years some of the recipes are no longer included,
and others appear that were connected to Lupoiu's new context:
the *RELAIS-PLAZA*, the *PLAZA ATHÉNÉE* [P.88], the *EXPO-COCKTAILS*,
and the *AIR FRANCE*...

After an introduction recounting the history of "mixes", beginning
in classical antiquity, came Lupoiu's precious recommendations
for making cocktails. From the primordial quality of the products
to the importance of ice—a good cocktail requires this just as a good
dish requires fire in the kitchen—here was advice from a twenty-
year career condensed in a few pages.

The cover illustration, by Géo Ausbourg, featured a blue and red
banner, plus three initials: A.B.F.

Lupoiu's advice, which stemmed from a desire to professionalize
his trade, opened the way for the Amicale des Barmen de France
(ABF), for which he served as president. The organization emerged
from the rupture with La Genevoise and its Barmen de France
section, from which Lupoiu had resigned, challenging the claim
that he had been ousted.[4]

Almost at the same time as the founding of the ABF, Marcel
Cacciolato, then in charge of the Plaza Athénée's Hall (as the hotel's
Conciergerie was called), wrote an eponymous book. For years
it served as a reference for the profession. Concerning the service
industry, it reflected on the need to adapt to progress,
to the development of business and tourism, to new technologies—
in other words, to modern times.[5]

The same motivations were at the origins of the ABF. *Cocktail "38"*,
the official publication of the organization published a few months
after it was founded, would be its echo.

---

[4] – La Genevoise, a cooperative of employees in the hotel industry, was founded
in Geneva in 1877. It had an international calling, and upon the initiative
of the Paris section, the United States section was founded in 1902.
The Barmen de France section within La Genevoise emerged in 1934.
*La Genevoise—Les Barmen de France*, monthly bulletin, No.12, March 1, 1938.

[5] – Pascal Payen-Appenzeller, *Hôtel Plaza Athénée* (Paris: Assouline, 2004).

The first class dining room of the *Normandie*.
Postcard issued by the Compagnie Générale Transatlantique French Line.

A cooperative association, the ABF would soon unite the entire French bar family and facilitate relationships with big brand representatives, always with the aim of developing tourism, which was key to the prosperity of one and all.[6]

On May 26, 1939, aboard the *Normandie*, Jean Lupoiu—head bartender of the Relais Plaza, founder and president of the ABF—left Le Havre for New York. Along with other bartenders, sommeliers, maîtres and chefs d'hôtel, all in charge of representing gastronomy at the French pavilion, he was heading for the New York World's Fair.
History repeating itself...

---

[6] – The first issue of the periodical was dated September 1938; the issues published the following year were named *Cocktail 39*. *Cocktail 38,* No.1, September 1938.

# THE ARTISTRY OF MIXING DRINKS
## FRANK MEIER, 1936

*"The man whose friendship is more courted
than that of many a president."*

Frank Meier at the bar of the Ritz, Paris, 1938.
Photo Roger Schall.

*"Possibly the best-known drink shaker
in the world."*

Frank Meier at the bar of the Ritz, Paris, 1938.
Photo Roger Schall.

The man and the bar, both legendary. Highly respected by his peers, lauded by his clients, Frank Meier was the forefather of the profession. He managed the Bar Cambon, commonly known as the Ritz Bar since its opening in 1921.

The Ritz Hotel was inaugurated in June 1898 by the man whom Edward VII nicknamed "the hotelier of kings and the king of hoteliers". From his native high-mountain pastures to the Place Vendôme, César Ritz's trajectory took him from Switzerland to the Côte d'Azur to London. Arriving in Paris in 1867 for the Universal Exposition, he would make his mark on every level of the restaurant profession and then on hotels— he quickly understood that a wealthy clientele required exceptional service.
Ritz first put that notion of excellence into practice while at the helm of the Grand Hôtel National in Lucerne and, later, at the Grand Hôtel in Monte Carlo. There, he hired Auguste Escoffier, because a great hotel must offer great cuisine. Together the two men would launch the modernization of the Savoy before heading to Paris. Part of the wave of new luxury hotels that popped up with each Universal Exposition, the one opened by César Ritz at 15, Place Vendôme was distinguished by the architect Charles Mewès's elegant splendor and refinements, with modern conveniences on every floor. For example, each room had its own full bathroom and telephone; each was lighted by electric bulbs, some hidden in what was the first indirect lighting. To 15, Place Vendôme was added number 17, and in the long hallway that separated the two buildings, shops were installed in an early version of a windowed arcade. The Ritz Hotel rivaled the excellence of *hôtels particuliers*, the grandest private estates. Marcel Proust stopped in daily because he felt at home.

In April 1921 the decision was made, under the auspices of Marie-Louise Ritz (widow of César, whose toned-down memoirs she would one day write)[1], to allot a space for American drinks on the hotel's rue Cambon side. That space would become Le Café Parisien, which was quickly known as Bar Cambon. You could enter via the Place Vendôme by crossing through tearooms and salons and then down the famous shopping arcade, or more simply via the rue Cambon, the "rue de la chance", as Coco Chanel liked to call it.

[1] – Marie-Louise Ritz, *César Ritz* (Paris: Éditions Tallandier, 1938).

Every morning, a long line formed right before noon, when the bar opened its doors. Immediately past the concierge, the bar was on the left and filled up in less than five minutes. The establishment was frequented by many journalists, the upper crust of the Anglo-American community, and gentlemen of the arts, politics, and business. It was a place solely for men. That is why, in 1926, the Café des Dames opened across the way; the name came from the term commonly used to designate the "waiting room" reserved for the fairer sex. This would become the Petit Bar when the Bar Cambon opened to women in 1936.
At the Bar Cambon, beneath murals by Maurice Pico (the same artist who had decorated the façade of the Folies Bergères), six bartenders officiated, all under the command of Frank Meier.

Born in in 1893 in Linz, Austria, Meier immigrated to America and learned the bar and hotel trade at the Hoffman House Hotel in New York, where the bar's reputation was as much attributable to its cocktails as to William-Adolphe Bouguereau's licentious painting *Nymphs and Satyr*, which hung on the wall and was covered by a drape.
From this hotel experience, Meier would draw a work ethic likely to meet the expectations of César Ritz. Meier designed the back of the bar, determining its organization right down to the arrangement of the bottles. He put together a team in which everyone had a clearly defined role: preparation, service, and the like. And above all, Meier wasn't behind the bar but in front of it, where he welcomed his clientele; he knew their preferences, provided information, and oversaw their well-being. In the luxury hotel world, the two most important men were henceforth the concierge, who welcomed those coming in from outside, and the bartender, who welcomed those coming in from within. A right-hand man, discreet and a polyglot, having traveled the world, Meier could provide the "custom" service and first-class cocktails (*BEE'S KNEES* [P.53], *OLYMPIC* [P.84], *GREEN HAT* [P.74], among others) that turned the Ritz Bar into an authority.
Training was important to Meier, so he lent his experience and perfectionism to other bartenders. Upon the initiative of the ABF, with Jean Lupoiu, he was an active honorary president. He was also a member of the International Bar Managers Association, which had its headquarters in New York.[2]

161

[2] — "Frank Meier est mort," *Le Club Hôtelier/Les Barmen de France*, No.18, (December 1947).

*The Artistry of Mixing Drinks* was published in 1936, during a period of political and social turmoil in France, a time that also launched a new but short belle époque for luxury hotels. The book was much more than a collection of recipes; it was a resource that contained the most varied kind of information, from the way to serve wine to different time zones, from a list of toxicides to a chronology of horseracing. A collection that turned cocktail preparation into true artistic talent.

Frank Meier and his team,
Bar Cambon, 1930.

# MADE IN FRANCE

## HERITAGE SPIRITS ENGAGE THE COCKTAIL

"They prepared an inventory of the aperitifs: the amaretto, the Junod absinthe, the Anis del Oso, which replaced the pre-war absinthe; the Byrrh, the quinquina, the Dubonnet, innocuous drinks; vermouth, Amer Picon, Cinzano, and so many other bottles, their many-colored splendor first pleasing the eye before tempting thirst."

Eugène Dabit, *L'Hôtel du Nord*, Paris, Denoël, 1929.

Bénédictine liqueur,
advertisement study, around 1930.

# COINTREAU
# "THE WORLDWIDE
# BRAND"

The Guignolet d'Angers was the first to preside over the success
of Cointreau Frères, a company founded by Édouard-Jean
and Adolphe in 1849 in that city. The cherry liqueur produced
in the convents of Anjou starting in the fifteenth century had
somewhat fallen out of favor. The brothers hoped to capitalize
on the rich regional production of various cherries and bring back
a taste for the liqueur.

Édouard (son of Édouard-Jean), who took over the company in 1875,
made it famous.[1] His awareness of consumer trends allowed him
to grasp the importance of advertising. Success was knocking
at the door. Having returned from a trip around the world,
he applied his same observations to the development of orange
peel liqueur (two bitter varieties, and three sweet) that he had just
invented and named triple sec.
Curaçao was already trendy (named for the Antilles island where
the Dutch made a liqueur from *bigarades* or bitter oranges), but
those liqueurs were not to Édouard's liking—too sweet! He wanted
to modify the "golden apple" taste to create an exceptional,
unmistakable liqueur, one unlike any being produced at the time.
It would be crystal clear, a tonic and a digestive. And it would come
in an amber bottle, bulky and square, that could stand on each
of its sides, a symbol of perfect balance. (To protect against fakes,
the model would be trademarked, with a red ribbon as the sign
of authenticity.)

Armed with this "visual tool", Édouard pursued his promotional
plan. In 1898 Pierrot, a character with a white-painted face
inspired by a photograph of the mime Raoul de Najac, became
the brand's image for its entire poster campaign. Pierrot featured
in Cointreau's advertising films, made just three years after
the Lumière brother's motion-picture projection. At the dawn
of the golden age of the automobile, there were also the first
promotional bottle-cars.

[1] – *Le Panthéon de l'Industrie*, No.592, July 25, 1886.

To distinguish itself from other triple sec brands on the market, the company's name was given first. The product would henceforth be called Cointreau liqueur.

After being initiated by Édouard, international growth became the priority of his two sons, who took the helm of the company in 1923 after the death of their father. André was in charge of production, and Louis took care of the commercial aspects. The slogan "La Marque Mondiale" (the worldwide brand) emerged at this time.

Although a distillery had opened in Canada in 1928 while the United States was in the throes of Prohibition, Louis launched the exportation of the liqueur to North America. Cases were transported by ship and then, upon nearing American shores, transferred to a smaller boat to dock discreetly. An American company that made casino chips took care of "distribution" through its network.

Cointreau liqueur quickly became an ingredient in many cocktails, the most famous being the *SIDE CAR* P.92 and the *WHITE LADY* P.100. The company promoted these new options, adding them to the liqueur's traditional preparation on ice. In its thick sales catalogue of November 1935, a specialty cocktail appeared: the *GRATTE-CIEL* P.74. Mixed and "bottled", it was sold in an elegant shaker.

*La Parisienne*. Advertisement, 1938.

# BYRRH
## "THE TONIC
## AND HYGIENIC WINE"

Brothers Simon and Palade Violet, traveling salesmen, settled
in Thuir, in the Pyrénées-Orientales region of southern France.
They opened a store where they sold fabric, drapes, wines,
and liqueurs. Developing the market for Spanish wines, including
Malaga, Simon invented a wine-based drink in 1866, which
he paired with different aromatic plants and cinchona bark. It would
be called Byrrh and the trademark registered in 1873. (Legend has
it that the name came from a random fabric order. Different fabric
categories and prices were referred to by capital letters, and the ones
for that client were B.Y.R.R.H.)

The "Malaga wine aperitif", the "cinchona aperitif", the "tonic
and hygienic wine"—whatever it was called, the liquid's fortifying
and stimulating qualities, promoted at a time when hygiene
was all-important, made it the benchmark of wine-based aperitifs.[1]
Byrrh was soon found in every establishment—cafés, bars, grocery
stores. It could be sipped straight, with water, or mixed into
a *BYRRH-CASSIS* [P.62] and, later, cocktails: *BYRRH* [P.60], *COCKTAIL
FRANCE* [P.69], *MASTER JACK* [P.82], and others. More than thirty million
bottles were sold annually in the early 1930s.

When Simon Violet died, in 1891, his son Lambert took over
direction of the company. Lambert developed the existing
infrastructure, expanded the storehouses, connected the factory
to train lines, and launched the shipping hall, a full-fledged station
where production was transported throughout France by truck.
With a marquee designed by Gustave Eiffel, the concourse came
to be known as the Gare Eiffel.
Lambert's widow, Marie, would head the company during
the Second World War, as would her children after her. The family's

168

[1]— Joseph Favre, *Dictionnaire Universel de cuisine et d'hygiène alimentaire*, vols. 1 and 2
(Paris: Librairie-imprimerie des Halles et de la Bourse du Commerce, 1889–91).
As for the "Jesuit powder" (so called because they brought it to Europe), composed
of cinchona bark, it was used therapeutically in France after the Englishman Talbot
used a mix of cinchona and Bourgogne wine for Louis XIV.

Byrrh advertisement, 1930s.

history was closely tied to the city that adopted it. The company took care of its own and engaged in forward-thinking social policies, granting personnel monthly family support per child, birth and death benefits, and paid annual vacations.[2] It sponsored the city's sports centers, and wine was henceforth purchased from local growers.

Such benevolence extended countrywide. Byrrh became the French aperitif of choice, bolstered by advertising in the press (from the 1903 poster contest published in *Le Monde Illustré* to ads in *L'illustration* by Georges Léonnec) as well as on the radio, on walls, and on the road (the company owned a fleet of 170 trucks plus promotional and business cars, all branded). Omnipresent in French life, Byrrh would henceforth sponsor all kinds of local and sporting events. Supporting rugby and soccer matches and the Tour de France, it also launched fishing championships, "the real sport of the masses". Aiming higher still, it offered customers an aviation "baptism" with free flying excursions on its private plane painted in company colors.

Despite economic difficulties at the end of the 1930s, the company set new goals. After building the world's biggest oak barrel in 1934, with a capacity of 420,500 liters, the plan was to fabricate a new tank for one million liters.

2 – *Quelques Vérités*, Byrrh brochure, Paris, 1938.

The dispatch hall, or Gare Eiffel.

Bénédictine advertising, 1934.

# BENEDICTINE
## "D.O.M."

Alexandre Le Grand was working as a wine and liquor merchant when in 1863, in a book of magic spells, he found the recipe for an elixir made by the monks of the Benedictine Abbey in the sixteenth century. He was able to re-create the drink and named it Bénédictine, in honor of the monastery. Le Grand became the official purveyor to the imperial court of Napoléon, and sales of Bénédictine broke one hundred thousand bottles annually in 1871. Moving out of the premises he had used until then, Legrand built a new distillery that would also be the image of the brand he had just created. He entrusted its construction to the architect Camille Albert, and the project was completed in 1888.

On the night of January 11, 1892, an act of arson ravaged the distillery woodshop of Bénédictine in Fécamp. The fire immediately spread through the entire building and was not brought under control until morning. The damage was considerable, but the laboratory where the distillery stood, as well as the museum and cellars, were saved. Nor were the production and distribution of the liqueur interrupted. Two people were arrested in connection with the crime and sentenced to a lifetime of forced labor at the French penal colony in Nouméa. Devastated by fire, it would be three more years before the "palace" devoted to Bénédictine would open definitively.

In no way did the building resemble a factory. A true castle in the neo-Renaissance style, it accommodated every stage of the liqueur's production. First, the laboratory and its distillation equipment; next to that, the barrels containing more than five hundred thousand liters of liqueur; downstairs, the cellars stored the eau de vie as well as the twenty-seven plants and spices that became ingredients in Bénédictine, its recipe a well-kept secret. On the floor above was the bottling area. The bottle, which to des Esseintes, the chief protagonist in Joris-Karl Huysmans' 1884 novel, *À rebours*, seemed "at once gently luxurious and vaguely mystical", was designed by Le Grand. Bottles were then corked and sealed in the labeling area and inscribed with *Véritable Bénédictine* and *Deo Optimo Maximo*, a Latin phrase meaning "To God, most good, most great." The sisters of the order of Saint Vincent de Paul oversaw operations while also managing the orphanage, which was sponsored by the company and where many female workers were raised. Then there was the shipping area where the bottles were packed into wood crates. As a precaution, the sawmill and woodshop were kept separate from the rest of the building. The palace was not only used for industrial purposes but also housed a museum for Le Grand's collection, which contained relics from the former abbey, art objects, furniture, and tapestries.[1] The museum and the rest of the buildings could be visited for the modest sum of 25 centimes.

Before the First World War, total sales of Bénédictine broke two million liters, with the main foreign markets being Russia and the United States. In 1918, however, sales fell to less than one million liters. During the war, many countries had adopted restrictions and protectionist measures regarding the importation of alcohol. The Russian Revolution in 1917, rapidly followed by a civil war, put an end to exports to the country. In the United States, Prohibition banned all sales of alcohol. Nevertheless, in 1928 the company created Arôme Bénédictine as a means of maintaining a presence on the market. It contained 6 percent alcohol and was promoted as a dessert condiment. The company quickly sought out new markets as well (the premise of its presence in Asia) and encouraged novel ways of consuming the drink, namely in cocktails. In 1936, at the 21 Club in New York, the *B&B* [P.50] cocktail (brandy and Bénédictine) was invented. The U.S. Bénédictine representative, Julius Wile Sons & Co., convinced the company to develop its own B&B, introducing the benefit of being aged in a barrel. Without delay the B&B brand, with its golden wax seal, was trademarked.

174

[1] – An illustrated catalogue of the museum's collection was published in 1888 by L. Durand et Fils.

The labeling room, under the supervision of nuns.

## CHARTREUSE
## "UNE TARRAGONE"

On April 29, 1903, the director-general of the French national
police set out to implement the Association Law of 1901, which
sought to limit the power (and the property) of large religious
institutions in France. Accompanied by squads of police officers
and soldiers, he proceeded to evacuate Grande Chartreuse.
Forced out of the monastery they had occupied since 1084
(the year the Carthusian order was founded at the foot
of the Chartreuse Mountains), the fathers took their secret
and sought refuge in Spain, where they opened a new distillery
in Tarragona.

Their secret was the recipe for an elixir that had been given
to the Carthusian monks by the Maréchal d'Estrées in Paris in 1605.
Because of the complexity of its formula—which calls for 130
plants—the monks passed it on to the head monastery, Grande
Chartreuse. It was there that the formula was perfected in 1735
and became the "plant elixir of the Grand Chartreuse". The recipe,
which has medicinal properties, was further tweaked to become
the green liqueur known as "Liqueur de Santé"; then in 1838 came
the yellow liqueur called the "Reine des Liqueurs". Sales were
managed by the monks and limited to the region. Officers posted
in the area tried the liqueur and took to it immediately; they soon
assumed responsibility for its distribution.
When the fathers were evicted in 1903, the French government
took ownership of the brand and marketed a Chartreuse liqueur,
but its only similarity was the name. Meanwhile, in Spain,
the monks continued to make and sell their liqueur under the name
"Tarragone". Starting in 1921, monks in Marseille began distilling
it once again in France.

Through a vast national advertising campaign called "Le Secret
de la Chartreuse", the liqueur's official representative finally
put an end to the imbroglio in 1929 after reaching an agreement

with the French government. A brochure was made available, free upon request, which helped readers distinguish between genuine Chartreuse, with its second label "Une Tarragone", from all other imitations. The brochure, which recounted the liqueur's history and identified a true bottle, also included a few recommendations. In addition to the traditional one-third green to two-thirds yellow mix were cocktails, including the *ALASKA* [P.48] and the *KOZACK* [P.78], both rather successful.

*Grande Chartreuse*, advertisement, 1934.

# FRENCH VERMOUTH

Vermouth comes from Italy—Turin, to be exact. In the eighteenth century, based on a traditional recipe, the brands Carpano and Cinzano perfected the combination of regional wines from the Piedmont by flavoring them with plants and spices and, later, sugar. Their success has never faltered.
Italian vermouth came to mean red and sweet, whereas French vermouth referred to a clear and dry version.

Joseph Noilly appreciated white wines that had a particular taste after being exposed to inclement weather. When transported by land or by sea, wines in open barrels were subject to changes in temperature and exposed to sun, rain, wind, and sea spray. In 1813, when he had a wine and spirits business in Lyon, Noilly invented his very particular vermouth. First, he let the wines age in open barrels, which were then left to macerate with plants and herbs.
In 1843 Noilly's son, who had joined the business, opened a branch in Marseille that was devoted to the production of vermouth. To run it, he chose Claudius Prat, who became his son-in-law and with whom he partnered to found the Noilly Prat company in 1855. After Marseille, it was in Marseillan, still along the sea, where the establishment would be dedicated to aging the wine used in vermouth. In response to growing demand, the company expanded over the years, buying more land and becoming so successful that it started exporting its product. At first limited to North Africa and the Mediterranean region, exports began shipping in the 1850s to the United States (mainly New York, San Francisco, and Louisiana). Next came Brazil and Argentina, Mexico and Cuba. Then Indochina, Hong Kong, and Australia and, finally, all the major trading and colonial ports, including London, Antwerp, and Amsterdam.

In Savoie, Joseph Chavasse, who owned a distillery in Les Échelles (the commune at the foothills of the Massif de la Chartreuse), was just back from a trip to Turin. He, too, wanted to create a vermouth that was tied to his region, one that combined the dry white wines of Savoie and the plants from surrounding mountains. His version emerged in 1821.

Living in Chambéry, his daughter Marie married Louis Ferdinand Dolin, who took the helm of the company when his father-in-law died. He gave it his own name, and thus Dolin Vermouth de Chambéry was established. As a widow, Marie crossed the Atlantic to participate in the Philadelphia World's Fair celebrating the centennial of the signing of the Declaration of Independence. She would return with a gold medal, and Vermouth de Chambéry became a benchmark in the industry. The trend was for Chambéry Fraise (vermouth and strawberry liqueur), which would lead the company to produce the Chambéryzette, a premixed aperitif. Vermouths de Chambéry proliferated, and in 1932 an appellation of origin was issued to protect local production and prevent imitations.

French vermouths had quickly become popular. So much so that soon a cocktail was including it as one of its main ingredients.

179

Bottles of Noilly Prat vermouth at the premises of Louis Noilly Fils & Cie,
Place Gerson, Lyon, 1937.

# SUZE
## "YOUR STOMACH'S FRIEND"

High in the Jura Mountains grows gentian, which can easily
be recognized by its large yellow flowers that spring from
the ground. The plant's roots, which have medicinal properties,
are deeply anchored into the soil. To cull gentian, one uses a long
two-pronged curved spade called the devil's fork. Once gathered,
the roots are transported fresh to the factory in Maisons-Alfort,
on the outskirts of Paris. There the roots undergo a process
that removes some of their bitterness but retains their fortifying
qualities as an aperitif and digestif. It is recommended to drink
the aperitif *SUZE* [P.95] straight in both winter and summer; you can
also add water, cassis, or lemon.

In 1889 Ferdinand Moureaux, at the helm of a struggling distillery,
had an idea for an aperitif that would not be based on wine—
distinguishing it from other existing brands—and that would
be both fresh and bitter. Gentiane Suze was born.
Gentiane Suze was the name commonly used until the early 1920s.
But by then the brand faced growing competition and imitations
proliferating on the market; among the serious contenders were
the Salers d'Auvergne and Avèse, which appeared in the 1930s,
as well as the most widely available imitation, the Gentiane Muse.
Henceforth, the name was Suze, inspired by Moureaux's
sister-in-law Suzanne Jaspart. For an aperitif, Moureaux would
always order, as per her wish, "the usual for Suze, a gentian".

The distinctive shape of the bottle, long with a short neck, would
be the subject of Picasso's 1912 collage *Verre et Bouteille de Suze*.
Originally about 75 proof (36 degrees GL), it would go down
to 40 proof after World War I. It was also during the 1920s that
Moureaux launched a wide-ranging advertising campaign,
when the brand's amber colors were painted on walls and facades
across France.

Suze is indeed your stomach's friend. Because it builds an appetite but limits over-indulgence, women in particular counted it among their favorites. But Suze is also, and always has been, the athlete's friend. Promoting its benefits, the brand became a sponsor of major sporting events. Production rose from 900,000 bottles in the 1920s to more than 13 million in the following decade. Its color is still that of a gentian flower and lends its name to the *YELLOW COCKTAIL* P.100.

Suze advertisement, 1934.

## "UN PERNOD!"

French society before the Great War was undermined by three
plagues: tuberculosis, syphilis, and alcoholism. This last
in particular decimated the working class and endangered society
as a whole with the violence and physical degeneration
that it engendered. Fingers pointed to the presumed guilty
party: absinthe.
This licorice-flavored spirit originated in Switzerland and was
derived from absinthe wormwood, to which was added fennel,
star anise, and green anise. It became popular among the bourgeoisie
before cheaper imitations of poorer quality infiltrated the masses.
Less expensive than wine, absinthe became the symbol
of alcoholism. The outbreak was caused by a form of addiction
to the "green poison", made all the more pernicious because
absinthe essence (used to make cheap versions) had just been
discovered to contain thujone, a chemical believed to cause
the dementia known as absinthism. Under pressure from anti-
alcohol groups and the winemaking monopoly, which saw
its market share fall in favor of the highly alcoholic beverage,
absinthe was officially banned by the French government
in March 1915.

Henri-Louis Pernod founded his distillery in Couvet, Switzerland,
in 1802; in 1805 he opened a second one in France, in Pontarlier.
His son Édouard managed the Swiss distillery, which focused
on exports, while Henri-Louis took care of the French market.
The consumption of absinthe initially spread in 1830 through
the French army, whose troops were then in North Africa where
absinthe, a curative, was used to "purify" water. Endowed with
military prestige, absinthe became the drink of the bourgeoisie
and bohemians, and consuming it involved a ritual that was just
as prestigious. The spirit was served diluted in lightly sweetened
water; at the time, there were absinthe fountains that dripped
water onto a sugar cube, which was placed on a spoon above

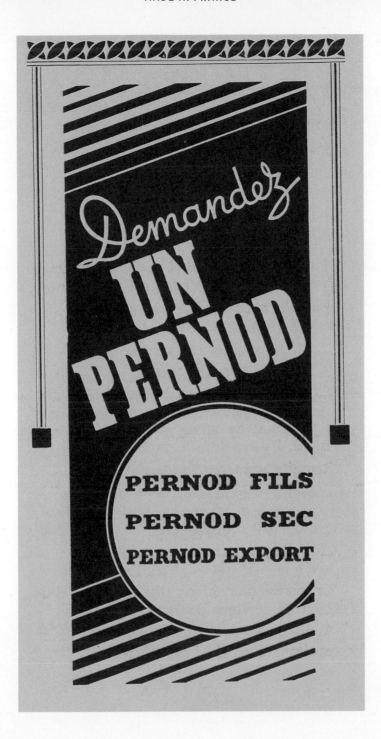

Pernod advertisement, 1930.

a glass containing absinthe. Pernod Fils became the brand name of quality absinthe. Picasso (he was everywhere), when developing his "series" of spirits, represented the bottle in his 1912 painting *Bouteille de Pernod et verre*.

Once the ban was lifted and management had instituted changes, Pernod Fils launched an anise-flavored aperitif in 1922, after the French government authorized the production of such liqueurs with a maximum 40 percent alcohol by volume. As a result, anise brands multiplied and had every ambition of replacing the defunct absinthe; even the ritual with the spoon remained intact. Yet despite the new competition, Pernod benefited from its reputation of prestige and high quality. The phrase "un Pernod" was trademarked, and if you used the company's name you had to be served its aperitif. In 1938 another decree authorized 45 percent alcohol by volume, motivating the company to produce its Pernod 45.

Many cocktail recipes still call for absinthe, but it is Pernod, more than its competition, that is used as a substitute. Between the forgotten *PERNOD MINT* and *PERNOD FLIP* and the popular *TOMATE*, the *SEAPEA* [P.92], one of Frank Meier's inventions, remains the classic of the genre.

*Franck Audoux came onto the food and cocktail scene by accident while studying for his master's degree in history. He has never looked back. After ten years as the director of a contemporary art gallery in Paris, Franck became a partner, manager and original member of the team behind Le Chateaubriand, which opened in April 2006, followed by Le Dauphin. He also founded a series of cocktail pairing events entitled "In Good Company", in which the creations of internationally renowned cocktail connoisseurs and bartenders are paired with food.*

*Having organized various bar-related events and worked on a number of editorial collaborations, in 2018 he opened CRAVAN, a cocktail bar/café in Paris's 16th arrondissement. Housed in a café built in 1911 by Hector Guimard, CRAVAN sees itself as a cross between a cocktail bar and a specialty café, focusing on quality in the glass, in the cup and on the plate. (Instagram: cravanparis)*

Cover of the book *L'Homme des Bars* by Louis Delluc,
La Pensée Française, Paris, 1923.

Alphonse Allais, *Le Captain Cap, ses aventures, ses idées, ses breuvages* (Paris: Juven, 1902).

Guillaume Apollinaire, *Alcools* (Paris: Mercure de France, 1913).

Louis Aragon, *Le paysan de Paris* (Paris: Gallimard, 1926).

Louis Aragon, *Aurélien* (Paris: Gallimard, 1944).

André Breton, *Nadja* (Paris: La Nouvelle Revue Française, 1928).

Louis-Ferdinand Céline, *Voyage au bout de la nuit* (Paris: Denoël et Steele, 1932).

Francis Carco, *Rue Pigalle* (Paris: Albin Michel, 1928).

Francis Carco, *Nuits de Paris* (Paris: Le Divan, 1927).

Jean Cocteau, *Les enfants terribles* (Paris: Grasset, 1929).

Colette, *La fin de Chéri* (Paris: Flammarion, 1926).

Eugène Dabit, *L'Hôtel du Nord* (Paris: Denoël, 1929).

Louis Delluc, *L'homme des bars* (Paris: La Pensée Française, 1923).

Pierre Drieu La Rochelle, *Le feu follet* (Paris: La Nouvelle Revue Française, 1931).

Robert Desnos, *Corps et bien* (Paris: Gallimard, 1930).

Léon-Paul Fargue, *Le piéton de Paris* (Paris: Gallimard, 1939).

André Gide, *Les faux-monnayeurs* (Paris: Gallimard, 1925).

Joseph Kessel, *Nuits de prince* (Paris: Les Éditions de France, 1927).

Valéry Larbaud, *Rues et visages de Paris* (Paris: Liège, 1927).

Michel Leiris, *L'âge d'homme* (Paris: Gallimard, 1939).

Pierre Mac-Orlan, *Le Quai des brumes* (Paris: Gallimard, 1927).

Raymond Queneau, *Les Enfants du Limon* (Paris: Gallimard, 1938).

Raymond Radiguet, *Le Diable au corps* (Paris: Grasset, 1923).

Maurice Sachs, *Alias* (Paris: Gallimard, 1935).

Maurice Sachs, *Au temps du Bœuf sur le Toit* (Paris: La Nouvelle Revue Critique, 1939).

Antoine de Saint-Exupéry, *Vol de nuit* (Paris: Gallimard, 1931).

Georges Simenon, *La tête d'un homme* (Paris: Fayard, 1931).

Georges Simenon, *Liberty Bar* (Paris: Fayard, 1932).

Philippe Soupault, *En joue!* (Paris: Grasset, 1925).

Philippe Soupault, *Les dernières nuits de Paris* (Paris: Calmann-Levy, 1928).

First published in the United States of America
by Rizzoli International Publications, Inc.
300 Park Avenue South, New York, NY 10010
www.rizzoliusa.com

*French Moderne: Cocktails from the 1920s & 30s.*
Copyright © Franck Audoux
For Rizzoli International Publications

**EDITOR**
Ian Luna

**PROJECT EDITOR**
Meaghan McGovern

**COPY EDITOR**
Mary Ellen Wilson

**PUBLISHER**
Charles Miers

**TRANSLATION**
Rebecca Cavanaugh
Molly Stevens

**BOOK DESIGN**
Cleoburo

**PRODUCTION**
Barbara Sadick
Susan Lynch

**ACKNOWLEDGMENTS**
The Editor would like to thank the following individuals and institutions for their crucial contribution:
Cléo Charuet, Marie Disle & Paul Icard

Front and back endpapers: TUNNEL P.96 cocktail, © Photographie Vavin
Back cover: Patrons at a "Bar Américain", Deauville, 1920s. Anonymous photograph.

*Printed in China*

2018 2019 2020 2021 2022/ 10 9 8 7 6 5 4 3 2 1
Library of Congress Control Number 2017959467
ISBN 978-0-8478-6160-6